Lipstick Forest
NEXT RIGHT

Fun with **Photoshop**®
Elements 3
Foto-Fakery for Everyone

Rhoda Grossman

SAMS   800 East 96th Street, Indianapolis, Indiana 46240

Fun with Photoshop® Elements 3

Copyright © 2005 by Sams Publishing

International Standard Book Number: 0-672-32730-9

Library of Congress Catalog Card Number: 2004095997

Printed in the United States of America

First Printing: February 2005

08   07   06   05   4   3   2   1

Trademarks

All terms mentioned in this book that are known to be trademarks or service marks have been appropriately capitalized. Sams Publishing cannot attest to the accuracy of this information. Use of a term in this book should not be regarded as affecting the validity of any trademark or service mark.

Adobe and Photoshop are registered trademarks of Adobe Systems Incorporated.

Warning and Disclaimer

Every effort has been made to make this book as complete and as accurate as possible, but no warranty or fitness is implied. The information provided is on an "as is" basis. The author and the publisher shall have neither liability nor responsibility to any person or entity with respect to any loss or damages arising from the information contained in this book.

Bulk Sales

Sams Publishing offers excellent discounts on this book when ordered in quantity for bulk purchases or special sales. For more information, please contact

U.S. Corporate and Government Sales
1-800-382-3419
corpsales@pearsontechgroup.com

For sales outside of the U.S., please contact

International Sales
international@pearsoned.com

Acquisitions Editor
Linda Bump Harrison

Development Editor
Jonathan A. Steever

Managing Editor
Charlotte Clapp

Project Editor
Andy Beaster

Production Editor
Benjamin Berg

Proofreader
Tonya Simpson

Indexer
Chris Barrick

Technical Editor
Doug Nelson

Publishing Coordinator
Vanessa Evans

Multimedia Developer
Dan Scherf

Interior Designer
Gary Adair

Page Layout
Eric S. Miller

Contents at a Glance

Table of Contents

About the Author

Rhoda Grossman is a cartoonist, illustrator, and painter who uses traditional and digital media in various combinations. She has co-authored several books on creative uses for Adobe Photoshop and Corel Painter with Sherry London. Rhoda created CD tutorials for Painter versions 6 through 8 without Sherry London. She has taught traditional drawing as well as computer graphics techniques at several brick-and-mortar institutions of higher (and wider) learning. As "Rhoda Draws a Crowd" she creates caricature entertainment (digitally and traditionally) for events from bar mitzvahs to international conventions. Check her out at **www.digitalpainting.com**.

Dedication

For my niece, Nesa, who continues the family tradition of being smart, funny, talented, Jewish, and short.

Acknowledgments

I'm grateful to the team of editors and designers at Sams who whipped this book into shape. I'm talking about Jon Steever, Andy Beaster, Ben Berg, Doug Nelson, and especially Linda Harrison. Linda, thanks for holding my hand whenever necessary and for the deadlines, which got me out of bed every morning. Thank you all for letting me use my own voice in this book, even when it was nasal and whiny.

To friends and family who provided images for me to play with, trusting me to use good taste and restraint: Rob Cook, Nancy Fox, Robert Gumpertz, Joy-Lily, Linda Kirby, Ida Levy, Mark Levy, Nesa Levy, Barbara Pollak, Gary Rowe, Jennifer Rozwood, Mark Shepard, Shura Wallin, and Woody Weingarten. I apologize for betraying your trust.

Thanks also to the companies whose stock images were provided for my use and abuse: Art Explosion, Corbis, BigFoto, RubberBall, and ShutterStock. In this category, my undying gratitude goes to Jon Oringer at ShutterStock.com, who saved me from a number of last-minute image emergencies.

Thank you, Sherry London, for your encouragement and support.

Most of all, I am grateful to the folks at Adobe Systems for coming up with a "light" version of Photoshop that's not just user friendly, it's positively chummy.

We Want to Hear from You!

As the reader of this book, *you* are our most important critic and commentator. We value your opinion and want to know what we're doing right, what we could do better, what areas you'd like to see us publish in, and any other words of wisdom you're willing to pass our way.

You can email or write me directly to let me know what you did or didn't like about this book—as well as what we can do to make our books stronger.

Please note that I cannot help you with technical problems related to the topic of this book, and that due to the high volume of mail I receive, I might not be able to reply to every message.

When you write, please be sure to include this book's title and author as well as your name and phone or email address. I will carefully review your comments and share them with the author and editors who worked on the book.

Email: graphics@samspublishing.com

Mail: Mark Taber
          Associate Publisher
          Sams Publishing
          800 East 96th Street
          Indianapolis, IN 46240 USA

Reader Services

For more information about this book or others from Sams Publishing, visit our website at www.samspublishing.com. Type the ISBN (excluding hyphens) or the title of the book in the Search box to find the book you're looking for.

Introduction

So, you wanna have fun with Photoshop Elements? You came to the right place. Do you want to create images that are beautiful, funny, or politically incorrect? Pull up a chair. If you want people to think you are on vacation in some exotic location while you're just hanging around the house, I'll show you how to fake the perfect postcard. If you'd like to make outrageous combinations of body parts, environments, or food, this book is for you. Are you dying to distort your spouse's face or make your parents look really old? This book can show you how, but maybe you need to work on anger management, too.

Who Are You?

You are a hobbyist, or recently retired, or a person with a demanding job who just wants to "unlax" creatively. You're a kid or a parent or a grandparent. You are a "shutterbug" who enjoys taking snapshots, or you have absolutely no interest in photography. You have an idea for an image that you need help creating, or you just want to fool around for a couple hours now and again. You definitely want to learn how to use Photoshop Elements as painlessly as possible. You are certainly a bargain hunter, proven by your purchase of Photoshop Elements at a small fraction of the cost of Photoshop CS, while getting about 90% of the features offered in the high-end version.

What Do I Need?

No experience with Photoshop Elements is necessary to start having fun right away, although you will probably work faster if you're an intermediate to advanced user. Appendix B, "Photoshop in a Peanut Shell," at the back of the book serves as a handy reference for basics you'll want to learn or be reminded of.

Although this book is written for Photoshop Elements 3, you can use an earlier version, and Photoshop CS users have not been ignored. There are tips where needed in a project (as well as in Appendix B) to point out any significant differences between the two programs.

Most Photoshop techniques can be performed just fine with a mouse, but there are a few that are much easier (and more fun!) with a Wacom tablet and pressure-sensitive stylus. A scanner will be handy, too, if you want to digitize old photos taken with a traditional film camera (remember those?).

Where Do I Start?

The chapters are self-contained and designed to be used in any order. Within a chapter it's a good idea to start with the first project and work down, but even that isn't absolutely required. So feel free to jump around and do what looks interesting at the moment.

Every project is liberally illustrated with images at various stages to keep you on track. Screen shots of palettes or dialog boxes are all done on an Apple computer, 'cause I don't do Windows. Except for cosmetic differences, these screen shots are identical to what their Windows counterparts would look like, and Photoshop Elements works exactly the same on both platforms. I'll give keyboard commands for both platforms, Mac first. For example: Command/Ctrl means use the Command key if you're on a Mac, the Control key if you do Windows.

What Will I Learn?

I made no attempt to cover every aspect of Photoshop Elements and I must say, with all due modesty, I was very successful. It turned out, however, that most of the important features of this amazing and versatile program got covered. If you do all the projects in all the chapters, you'll have a good grasp of most Photoshop techniques and at least a nodding acquaintance with many others. When you finish *Fun with Photoshop Elements 3* and want to continue your adventures in image manipulation, there are resources listed in Appendix A, "Resources," to help you do just that.

Where's the CD?

You won't find a CD to accompany this book on the inside back cover, or anywhere else. We wanted to keep the cost as low as possible and pass the savings on to you. The source images needed for most of the projects are available for download from the *Fun with Photoshop Elements 3* website at www.samspublishing.com. Type the book's ISBN (0672327309) in the Search field to find the page you're looking for.

Here's where you'll find pictures of people, places, and things created by professionals and obtained from stock photography companies. ShutterStock.com has been especially generous. You'll also find some "unprofessional" images donated by my family and friends. For some projects you'll have access to exactly the same images I worked with, and in other cases reasonably similar photos are provided. Many projects can and should be done with your own photos. Wouldn't you much rather distort the faces and bodies of your family rather than some total stranger? See Appendix A for more info on image resources.

Legal Stuff

If you scan images printed in books or magazines or search the web for digital pictures, be aware that such items might be copyright protected. That's not a problem unless you want to publish your edited versions. Copyright law gives the original creator of an image all rights to it, including derivations thereof (or is it "wherefrom"?). How much would you have to change an image to make it legally your own and not just a derivation? Are you willing to go to court to find out?

When it comes to using the likeness of a celebrity, things can get complicated. Are you infringing on the copyright of the subject or the photographer who created the photo? Maybe both! Famous people have the "right of publicity" to prevent others from making money with their likeness, even after death. On the other hand, ordinary folks have the right to privacy, so you need to get a "model release" signed before you can legally publish their face.

There are exceptions to copyright protection, called *fair use*. For example, you can publish doctored images of famous people for satirical purposes. How about drawings? As a professional caricature artist I need to publish examples of my work, using famous faces to demonstrate my skill. Not a problem, legally…unless it's Jay Leno. He's kinda prickly about stuff like that, maybe 'cause he's such a popular target. Anyhow, some of my colleagues have gotten "cease and desist" suggestions from Leno's staff. 'Nuff said.

Copyright expires 70 years after the death of the creator, at which time the image becomes *public domain*, so anything goes. An image like the Mona Lisa is *way* in the public domain, even though the painting itself is owned by the Louvre in Paris. Ownership of a piece of art is completely separate from usage rights thereto.

The images made available to you on the *Fun with Photoshop Elements 3* website are provided only for your personal use in working the projects. All other rights are reserved by the copyright holders.

I'm glad we had this little chat. Now, go have fun with Photoshop!

Project 1:
**The Forest and
the Trees**

Project 2:
Replace the Face

Project 3:
Making Faces

Project 4:
Body Transplants

Project 5:
Antelope, Schmantelope

Chapter 1

The Old
Switcheroo

We'll create seamless composites by swapping parts of one image with another. This is a great way to make an image that is more than the sum of its parts.

Project 1: **The Forest and the Trees**

Figures 1.1 and 1.2 show a couple of nature photos that are not as interesting as they could be. A blend of both will be more exciting, even if not exactly true to life. Yeah, I know it's not right to fool Mother Nature.

1. Open **forest.jpg** and **sunrise.jpg**. The forest photo needs more contrast or a greater range of values. This pic is easily and dramatically improved using one or more Enhance commands. Try Auto Levels or Auto Contrast. Figure 1.3 shows Auto Levels applied to the left side and Auto Contrast to the right side, so you can see the difference. Apply the Enhance effect you like. Now we're ready to paste the forest into the black foreground of the sunrise (or is it a sunset? I'm a city gal).

2. With **sunrise** as the active image, choose the Magic Wand tool. Increase Tolerance (in the Tool Options bar) from the default 32 to about 60, and uncheck the Contiguous option.

3. Click in the dark foreground of the image. All pixels that fall within the tolerance should be selected. To add the orange glow on the middle tree to the selection, just hold the Shift key down and click on the pixels you want to include. Figure 1.4 shows the "marching ants" selection.

4. Make **forest** the active image and Select All (Cmd/Ctrl+A).

Figure 1.1
The Black Forest. (Photo courtesy of Joy-Lily.)

Figure 1.2
Woodsy wallpaper. (Photo courtesy of Joy-Lily.)

Want to try bringing out some detail in the dark foreground of the sunset image? Use Enhance, Auto Smart Fix. The result is greater clarity of dust, streaks, and scratches! You were better off with a solid black. Use Edit, Undo. You'll be needing Undo a lot, so learn the keyboard shortcut to save time: Command/Ctrl+Z.

Fix it? Fuhgeddaboudit!

Figure 1.3
Two enhancements for the price of one.

5. Use Edit, Copy (Cmd/Ctrl+C). Now the forest image is ready to be pasted wherever you like.

6. Return to **sunrise**, where the selection you made is still active. If not, repeat step 2.

Figure 1.4
Ants marching through the forest.

7. Use Edit, Paste Into Selection. In Figure 1.5 the forest nearly fills the black foreground area of the sunrise photo. Cool, huh?

Adjust the Size or Position

All that's left to do is adjust the size or position of the forest. It was not quite wide enough to fill the entire sunrise foreground.

8. Switch to the Move tool (top of the toolbar) and enable Show Bounding Box in the Options bar. You'll now see "handles" for dragging both sides of your pasted forest to match the size of the sunrise.

9. Choose Image, Transform, Distort so you can drag each corner of that bounding box around independently. Experiment with different sizes and angles until you like the results. Figure 1.6 shows a vertical stretch, and Figure 1.7 has a slight rotation.

Figure 1.5   **Instant detail.**

Figure 1.6   **Tweaked to perfection.**

Figure 1.7   **Enough, already. Just pick one.**

Project 2: **Replace the Face**

When my friend Nancy sent me this photo of a monkey and its baby, I knew exactly what was needed. Once again, in Figure 1.8, there is a black area with no detail where the face should be. So, let's place a face. This smiling man from Figure 1.9 will do for now, but feel free to use a family member or high-ranking public official.

Figure 1.8
Monkey without a face.
(Photo courtesy of Nancy Fox.)

Figure 1.9
Face without a monkey.
(Photo courtesy of RubberBall.com.)

The man's face is much too big and he's facing the wrong way. Let's fix that.

1. Use Image, Resize, Image Size and enter 1 inch for width in the Document Size field. Click OK to confirm the change and dismiss the dialog box.

2. Use Image, Rotate, Flip Horizontal.

Transferring the Face

That's close enough for now. You'll tweak the size and position of the face after it's pasted into the monkey.

Figure 1.10   **If the face fits....**

3. Open the monkey image and choose the Magic Wand tool. Use the default **32** for Tolerance and be sure to enable the Contiguous option so you don't select dark pixels all over the image. Click in the dark face space.

4. Use Select, Feather to make the edge of the selection "soft." A Feather radius of five pixels should do nicely.

5. Return to the human image and use the Rectangular Marquee tool to select the face from chin to hairline.

6. Use Edit, Copy to prepare the face for pasting.

7. Target the monkey image and use Edit, Paste Into Selection.

8. Use Image, Transform, Free Transform (Cmd/Ctrl+T) to get the angle and placement of the face just right.

9. Let's reduce the saturation of the face in Figure 1.10. Choose the Sponge tool, which shares a room with the Dodge and Burn tools. Be sure to use Desaturate Mode in the Options bar. Flow at 50% and brush size 65px is fine. Now just paint over the face in one continuous stroke.

TIP

In Photoshop CS the Paste Into command gives you a new layer. With Elements there is no layer, so you'll have to use Transform maneuvers while the selection is still active. When your cursor looks like a curved double-headed arrow, you can drag to rotate. To drag one corner in or out, hold down the Command/Ctrl key first. When you're finished with the transform, press the Return key to commit.

Figure 1.11 shows one proud primate papa.

Figure 1.11   **Takin' care of monkey business.**

Here's how to make the transition from face to fur smoother. After making the Magic Wand selection in step 3, Select, Modify, Expand by about 5 pixels. This adds some of the fur around the face to your selection. Now choose a larger feather amount, about 12 pixels. Paste the human face into the selection, as before. Apologies to my friend Linda, who asked for a virtual face lift. I don't think this is what she had in mind.

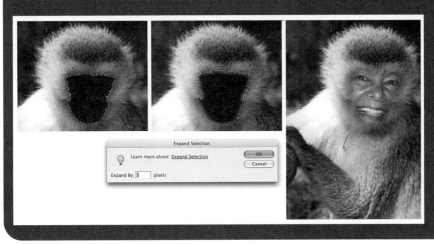

Project 3: **Making Faces**

The human face is capable of an incredible variety of expressions. Facial features can be combined in an infinite number of ways…well, enough ways to keep you entertained for a couple of hours at least. Let's reshuffle some face parts.

Figure 1.12 shows a redheaded kid with a goofy expression. I'll make him look even goofier. Use a photo of your own to make this more fun. Figure 1.13 shows my collection of face parts created from photos of people with different ages, races, and gender. This file, faceparts.psd, is available for download from the *Fun with Photoshop Elements 3* website. Each facial feature is on its own layer, making it very easy to switch them to other images.

Figure 1.12
Professional model— don't try this at home.
(Photo courtesy of RubberBall.com.)

1. Use the Move tool (V) to click on the eye at the upper-left corner of the face parts collection. Drag and drop it onto the kid's face. Copy and paste works just as well.

   Figure 1.14 shows the Layer palette along with the new eye layer. I tilted it slightly, as you can see from the angle of the bounding box. The eye was pre-feathered and the color match is darned good, so it blends nicely into the face. Now he isn't squinting, but winking.

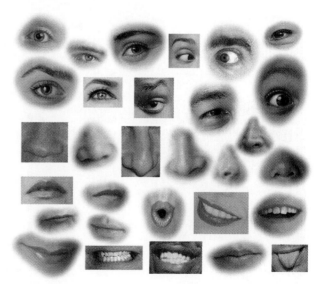

Figure 1.13
More fun than Mr. Potato Head.

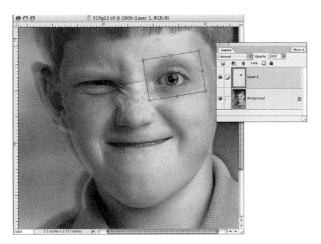

Figure 1.14   **A wink is as good as a nudge.**

Figure 1.15   **Red shift.**

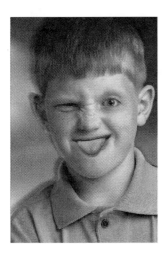

Figure 1.16
Your face could freeze like that.

Create a Composite

It's fairly easy to make a seamless composite when the two images have similar lighting and skin tones. If they don't, Photoshop has ways to help fake it.

2. Drag and drop the mouth from the lower-right corner of the collection to the boy. The angle is fine, but you'll need to make it bigger by dragging from one or more of the handles on the bounding box.

3. Use the Eraser tool (E) to blend the hard edges of the layer into the background. Work carefully, adjusting brush size and opacity as needed.

Match the Skin Tones

The mouth and tongue are too blue for the face. In the next step we'll match the skin tones.

4. From the Layer menu at the top of the screen, choose New Adjustment Layer, Hue/Saturation. Click on the Group with Previous Layer check box to select it. This will restrict the adjustment to the mouth layer. Move the Hue slider to the right, toward red and away from blue, to a value of **+15**. Increase *saturation*, the richness of color, to about **+20**. The Hue/Saturation dialog box with those changes is in Figure 1.15.

Figure 1.16 shows the finished image. If you want to work with tongues some more, and are willing to admit it, check out Chapter 2, "Now You See It, Now You Don't."

Project 4: **Body Transplants**

Wonder how you would look as a supermodel or Hollywood hunk? Let's spare my friend Woody in Figure 1.17 some serious workout sessions and hormone injections by just giving him virtual muscles.

For this project you'll have more fun working with your own photos. Try to find two images whose skin tones and lighting are reasonably similar. Let's call these images "head" and "body."

1. Open the head image. If you need to, use Image, Rotate, Flip Horizontal to get the head facing the other direction.

2. Open the body image. Drag and drop the head to the body, making a new layer. Resize and maneuver it into place, just like in the monkey exercise. Turn the layer opacity down temporarily to about **50%**, as in Figure 1.18, so you can confirm the size and position of the head layer. Not a bad way to see a hybrid blend of two faces!

3. Return Opacity to 100%. To begin getting rid of the head's background, use the Magnetic Lasso tool to trace loosely around the edges of the head and beard. The Magnetic Lasso senses edges, but you won't get a perfect selection in this case.

Figure 1.17
Heads, you lose.
(Photos courtesy of Nancy Fox and ShutterStock.com.)

Figure 1.18
Dragged and dropped on his head.

The Magnetic Lasso shares space on the toolbar with the standard Lasso and the Polygon Lasso. It creates a path of points that becomes a selection marquee when you double-click. For this example I used 5px for Width, 10% for Edge Contrast, and 100 for Frequency.

4. Use Select, Modify, Expand by 3 or 4 pixels, to minimize the amount of hair you might have missed.

5. Use Select, Inverse to select the pixels outside the face instead of the face itself. Press the Delete/Backspace key. Deselect.

6. We can see in Figure 1.19 that the head needs to be nudged a bit to the right to match up better with the body's neck. *Nudge* means choose the Move tool and use the keyboard arrows to move an item a tiny amount.

7. Use the Background Eraser to get rid of the unwanted pixels under Woody's beard. This dandy tool shares space on the Tool strip with the standard Eraser. Stroke the tool just outside the edge of the beard. The center "hot spot" will remove pixels of a similar color, sensing the edge. Use the default Tolerance of **50%** and tweak if needed.

8. The yellow pixels remaining around Woody's hair will have to go. Luckily, they are about the same value (brightness) as the new blue sky background. (You'll see where I'm going with this). Use the Eyedropper tool to establish that sky blue as the foreground color.

9. Choose the Brush tool and select Color Mode from the pop-up list in the Options bar. Color Mode lets you replace color without changing value. Paint that "halo" of yellow, with some variations in the opacity setting for more realism.

Figure 1.19 **Place the face.**

10. Switch to Normal mode for the Brush and highlight the background image (the body) in the Layer list. You're still using sky blue, right? Paint over any dark hair from the original hunk's head. Sample the darker blue at the horizon and the water to paint out the clump of hair at his neck.

Does your new and improved Woody look like Figure 1.20?

Figure 1.20
Now hand me the Grecian Formula.

There were some pretty sophisticated techniques in this exercise. Ya done good. So, as a treat, check out the first image. This is how I looked about 15 years ago with skinny thighs (yeah, right!). The second image shows how I expect to look in another 5 years if this book doesn't do well.

Author's fantasy.

Author's nightmare.

Project 5:   Antelope, Schmantelope

You can assure any animal rights activists who come after you that all species in this exercise were treated humanely.

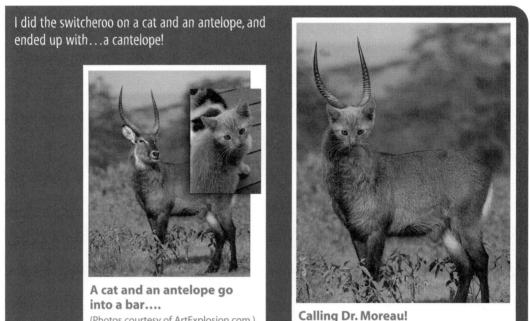

I did the switcheroo on a cat and an antelope, and ended up with...a cantelope!

A cat and an antelope go into a bar....
(Photos courtesy of ArtExplosion.com.)

Calling Dr. Moreau!

Figure 1.21   **One of them is a symbol for the USA.**
(Photos courtesy of ArtExplosion.com.)

Figure 1.21 invites us to cross an eagle with a lizard.

I. Open **Eagle.jpg**. Selecting the eagle's head is easy, because there is a strong contrast with the dark background. The Magic Eraser is the ideal tool for eliminating background pixels. (It shares a space with the standard Eraser and the Background Eraser.) Just click a few times in the dark areas and all similar pixels will magically disappear! Be sure to have "contiguous" checked in the options bar, so you don't remove dark pixels around the eye. I lowered Tolerance to 24, so I wouldn't remove any dark pixels in the lower beak.

2. Use the standard Lasso tool to make a loose selection around the head, as shown in Figure 1.22. No need to have a tight fit, because the head is surrounded by transparency (that's what the gray and white checkerboard means.)

3. Open **Lizard.jpg**. Use the Move tool to drag-and-drop the eagle's head to the lizard image. Resize and position as needed.

4. There's a little bit of lizard showing above the eagle's head. Let's clone it out. Activate the background in the Layer list. Place the Clone Stamp tool above and to the left of the offending lizard pixels. Press the Option/Alt key and click. This establishes the source pixels for the next step.

5. Move your cursor over the lizard pixels and paint.

6. Try an alternative blending mode to change the way the head layer interacts with the background. I chose Hard Light (see Figure 1.23) to get some of the scaliness of the lizard to show through, especially around the eye. Now let's try to find a country to adopt Figure 1.24 as its national symbol.

Figure 1.22   **Natural selection.**

Figure 1.23
A Hard Light to follow.

Figure 1.24   **A mascot in search of a team.**

Here are two additional specious species spliced together for your amusement, and mine. Behold the "eleopard" in the first image and the "cheebird" in the second image. You can download similar source images from the *Fun with Photoshop Elements 3* website.

A carnivore that never forgets.
(Photos courtesy of ArtExplosion.com.)

I can perch anywhere I want!
(Photos courtesy of ArtExplosion.com.)

Project 1:
Colorful Tongues

Project 2:
**Gone But Not
Forgotten**

Project 3:
**Out of Africa—
Completely**

Project 4:
Protective Coloration

Chapter 2

Now You See It,
Now You Don't

Based on the design principle that "Less Is More," you'll learn to remove people from a photo. Practice on images available for download from the *Fun with Photoshop Elements 3* website, and then take your "ex" out of all the family pictures. You'll also help a frog blend into his environment and cure a rare disease. What a chapter!

Project 1: **Colorful Tongues**

Figure 2.1 shows two kids and their grandpa suffering from blue-tongue disease, a rare disorder that runs in families. There's no known cure, although we can relieve the symptoms with the application of Photoshop.

1. Open **bluetongue.jpg**, shown in Figure 2.1. Let's give the kid on the left a normal tongue. Use the Eyedropper to sample a healthy pink color from the tip of his earlobe.

2. Choose the Brush tool (B) and select Color from the pop-up Mode list in the Options bar.

3. Paint over the tongue with the brush at about **80%** opacity. Reduce opacity to about **40%** and use a smaller brush size to paint the bluish parts of the teeth and gums.

Figure 2.1
Speaking in tongues. (Photo courtesy of Nancy Fox.)

Figure 2.2 shows the cured tongue. (Hmm, why do I have a craving for a deli sandwich?)

Cure one disease and create another affliction. Give the second kid severe cyanosis by painting his whole face blue in Color mode at 100%. As for Grandpa, he's got jaundice after being painted yellow at about 50% opacity. That "banana slug" tongue was painted at 100%.

Off-color joke.

Figure 2.2
Healthy tongue, stupid T-shirt.

Project 2: **Gone But Not Forgotten**

Notice the fellow in Figure 2.3. Those sideburns tip us off that this photo was shot in the '70s. Let's take him completely out of the picture and cover him seamlessly with San Francisco Bay and the city skyline.

1. Open **FriscoTwo.jpg**. Use the Rectangular Marquee tool to select the sky, city, and water on the left side of the image. The lower edge of the selection should line up with the top of the woman's head. Don't include the boat at the left edge of the picture. See Figure 2.4.

Figure 2.3
California couple. (Photo courtesy of Rob Cook.)

Figure 2.4
A most excellent selection!

2. Edit, Copy followed by Edit, Paste will
    make a new layer, **Layer 1**. The image
    won't look any different until you drag
    the layer to the right with the Move
    tool (see Figure 2.5).

3. Click on Background in the layer list
    and make a rectangular selection of
    sky and water on the right side.

4. Copy and paste as before, and move
    this Layer 2 over to cover the rest of
    our guy's head. Obvious seams are
    showing in Figure 2.6, and we'll take
    care of those later.

5. Do another select, copy, and paste
    sequence for a rectangle of water at
    the left, bounded by the boat and the
    woman's shoulder.

Figure 2.5
Peek-a-boo!

Figure 2.6
I left my head in Sausalito.

Figure 2.7
Three layers—groovy!

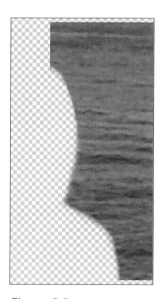

Figure 2.8
Remains of the bay.

6. Move this new Layer 3 to the right edge of the image, as in Figure 2.7.

7. Use the Eraser tool (E) to remove the pixels on Layer 3 that cover up the woman. It will be necessary to reduce the opacity of the layer while you work, and helpful to zoom in to a higher magnification. Reduce brush size as you get closer to the edges of her hair and sweater, and reduce opacity of the Brush to create a soft edge. Figure 2.8 shows how my Layer 3 looks after erasing is complete, with visibility of the Background and other layers turned off. Visibility is toggled on and off with the eyeball icons in the Layers palette.

ZOOMING IN AND OUT—FAR OUT!

Among the many timesaving keyboard shortcuts common to all versions of Photoshop and Photoshop Elements are Command/Ctrl + (plus sign) to zoom in, or Command/Ctrl - (minus sign) to zoom out. Also very handy are the bracket keys to change brush size (left bracket makes brush smaller, right bracket makes it larger—just ask Alice). Opacity changes for tools can be made quickly with number keys: for example, press "5" for 50%, zero for 100%.

8. Merge all layers into the background with the Flatten Image command in the Layers palette pop-up menu.

Exorcise De-Man

There are only a few bits and pieces of the fellow still showing. We'll get rid of those and the telltale seams using the Clone Stamp tool.

9. Choose the Clone Stamp tool (S). Let's get rid of the blue denim knee at the bottom left of the picture and that black stuff behind it by cloning some water over it. Disable the Aligned option and Option/Alt click about halfway between the knee and the left edge of the image.

10. Start painting close to the sweater and outward. You'll probably need several strokes, and you might have to click for a new source pixel once or twice.

TIP

Keep your eye on the moving crosshairs, showing you exactly where your pixels are coming from. When that "hot spot" gets close to the edge of the image, you're about to run out of pixels.

11. Clone water over the remains of our guy's hand at the lower right and that oddly shaped remnant of his shirt collar over the woman's head. Change the source pixel as needed and lower the opacity of your tool to avoid any obvious repeating patterns in the water. Figure 2.9 shows the lower part of the image completed.

There are two keys to using the Clone Stamp effectively: (1.) your choice of source pixel, which you establish by clicking on the desired spot while holding down the Option/Alt key, and (b.) whether you use the Align option. With Align enabled, each stroke you paint is offset from the source pixel. When the Align option is disabled, every stroke begins on the original source pixel. If that was clear as mud, this image should help.

I've got Align on you.

I made an Option/Alt click on the tongue with the Clone Stamp tool. Then I painted three strokes. The left half of the example shows the results with Aligned turned on. On the right side I painted three strokes with Aligned turned off, so every stroke begins with the tongue. I feel much better now that we've had this little talk. Someday you'll thank me. And now, back to our project.

Figure 2.9
Alone at last!

Figure 2.10
"I thought he'd never leave!"

Remove the Seams

Finally, we'll eliminate the unsightly seams in the sky and water. The same cloning maneuvers will help re-create a convincing San Francisco skyline.

12. Create a smooth transition in the sky and avoid a repeating "wallpaper" pattern in the city buildings. As you work, remember you have the following variables to change as needed:

   - The source pixel
   - Alignment on or off
   - Opacity
   - Brush size

   Figure 2.10 shows the finished piece. It's not perfectly flawless, but it's close enough.

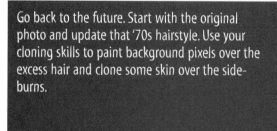

Go back to the future. Start with the original photo and update that '70s hairstyle. Use your cloning skills to paint background pixels over the excess hair and clone some skin over the sideburns.

I'll leave shaving in your initials up to you

Project 3: **Out of Africa— Completely**

In Figure 2.11, my friend Nancy is posing with a Massai warrior on her recent trip to Kenya. Suppose we're preparing a book on African dress and body decoration. Any excuse to use our Photoshop skills to wipe Nancy out.

Let's examine the image and consider strategy. There's no overlap between the figures. Except for two points where their clothes are barely touching, we won't have to be concerned about cloning carefully to the edge of the warrior. That makes things much easier than our project with the California couple.

There are a great variety of background materials to clone from: dirt, grass, rocks, tree trunks, leafy stuff. Better yet, there is plenty available on both sides as well as above and below the figures. Our task, essentially, is to be landscape architects. So, let's plunge into the jungle. The following steps are just suggestions:

1. Open **Africa.jpg**. Choose the Clone Stamp tool and begin covering Nancy with background elements from the right side of the image. Avoid noticeable pattern repeats, what I call the "wallpaper" effect. That patch of dirt and grass over Nancy's legs in Figure 2.12 is a good example of a pattern repeat that needs fixing.

Figure 2.11
Ebony and Ivory. (Photo courtesy of Nancy Fox.)

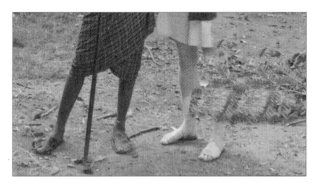

Figure 2.12
Wallpaper on the ground?

2. Use Option/Alt-click to establish the source pixels in the patch of grass on the left side of the image. Clone over the problem area near Nancy's legs.

3. Continue using cloning techniques to eliminate Nancy completely.

4. The light brown tree and bright green tree that were showing above Nancy's head now look like they are floating in mid-air. Decide whether to clone more of those trees downward or to cover that area with foliage from the left of the warrior's head. Figures 2.13 and 2.14 show both solutions.

Figure 2.13
If a tree floats in the forest and there's no one to hear it...

After you clone Nancy out, clone some more warriors in. Option/Alt click on the Massai tribesman and paint (with Aligned selected) on a new layer. You can resize and duplicate the layer copy any number of times. Erase as needed to show them behind trees or bushes.

The trouble with tribals.

Figure 2.14
Bring me a shrubbery!

Project 4: **Protective Coloration**

The frog in Figure 2.15 is just asking for trouble. Bright red against a green and gray background? Can you say "predator?" Let's give this little amphibian the ability to mimic his environment so he can live to (uh) croak another day.

1. Choose the Brush tool (B) and select Color from the pop-up list of painting modes in the Options bar.

2. Use the Eyedropper to sample a green color from the upper part of the background.

ANOTHER SHORTCUT FOR LAZY PEOPLE

When you are working with the Brush tool, you don't have to go back to the Tools palette to use the Eyedropper. Simply hold down the Option/Alt key and your cursor becomes the eyedropper icon. Click to sample a color and release the modifier key. You're ready to paint.

Figure 2.15
Does this color make me look fat? (Photo courtesy of ArtExplosion.com.)

3. Paint the upper part of the frog at **100%** opacity. Color mode lets you replace color without changing tonal value.

4. Sample a gray from the rock under the frog and paint the lower part of the frog. (Painting with gray in Color mode is the same as using the Sponge tool in Desaturate mode.)

5. Sample another green and reduce opacity of the brush. Paint a gradual color transition on the frog. Our frog acts like a chameleon in Figure 2.16.

Figure 2.16
Don't make me work with plaid!

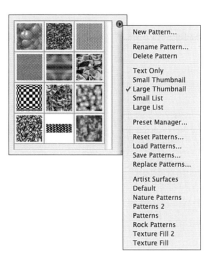

Figure 2.17
Show me something in paisley.

Subtle Color/Texture Variation

We can do better than that. We can create more subtle color variations and textures using the Pattern Stamp tool.

The Pattern Stamp shares a space with the Clone Stamp. Pattern Stamp allows you to paint with your choice of pattern. There are several sets of patterns available in the Pattern pop-up menu on the Options bar, shown in Figure 2.17. Rather than search for patterns, we'll make our own.

1. Choose the Rectangular Marquee tool. Make a selection in the green background as shown in Figure 2.18.

2. Edit, Define Pattern from Selection. You'll need to name the new pattern. I called mine "mottled green." It will now be available in the current Pattern Picker.

3. Choose the Pattern Stamp tool. Find and activate your new pattern from the Pattern Picker. Choose Color in the Painting Mode list and **100%** opacity in the Options bar. Paint the upper half of the frog. Notice the subtle variations in hue.

Figure 2.18
The latest thing in "Forest Blur."

4. Make a new pattern from the gray rock. Select an area with some hue variation. Figure 2.19 shows an ideal selection.

5. Repeat step 3 with your new pattern and paint the lower half of the frog. Reduce opacity to create a smooth transition between the green and gray sections of the frog, as shown in Figure 2.20.

Change of Scenery?

Okay, so now you've got a critter that can hide successfully in the jungle or on a rock. But what if he needs to disappear into a pile of heart-shaped candy? I thought you'd never ask.

1. Open the original frog image and **candyhearts.jpg**.

2. Enhance, Adjust Color, Remove Color to completely desaturate the frog image.

Figure 2.19
Will this go with my tweed suit?

Figure 2.20
Now I need new shoes and a matching handbag.

FEAR OF COMMITMENT

If you want to be able to bring back some or all of the color later, use an Adjustment Layer for Hue/Saturation. Set the Saturation slider to -100. Adjustment Layers are great for keeping your options open, ideal for people who have a hard time making decisions.

Figure 2.21
Amphibious valentine?

3. Drag and drop the candy hearts onto the frog, where it makes a new Layer, as in Figure 2.21. Use Free Transform (Command/Ctrl+T) and pull the corners of the bounding box until the layer is large enough to cover the background.

4. Set the Blending Mode of the layer to Vivid Light. Try some other blending modes, as long as you're up.

5. I like the way the frog and the candy layer interact in Vivid Light mode, but the combination is way too saturated. Layer, New Adjustment Layer, Hue Saturation will fix that. Reduce saturation to taste. Figure 2.22 shows your Layer palette at this point, and Figure 2.23 is the final image.

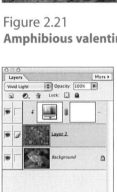

Figure 2.22
So many blending modes, so little time.

Figure 2.23
Froggy went a-courtin'.

The Gradient tool (just below the Paint Bucket) uses blending modes, too. Choose Color mode, Linear style, and the Violet, Orange preset. Drag vertically from the top of the image to the bottom. Instantly create a frog with matching environment, or an environment with frog to match.

Blending in thanks to blending modes.

Project 1:
**A Younger You in
Minutes**

Project 2:
Fast Forward

Project 3:
**Who's the Tallest
of Them All?**

Chapter 3

Mirror, Mirror,
Off the Wall

So you'd like to bring the
blush of youth back to your
cheeks, whiten your smile, and
squeeze your crow's feet into
a size five again? Photoshop
can improve your image. I'm
afraid it can't do much for
your shallow personality and
obsession with superficial
appearances. Step up for a
facelift with no scars, no pain,
and—best of all—no outra-
geous medical fees.

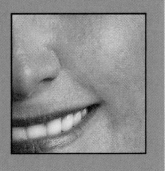

Project 1: **A Younger You in Minutes**

The middle-aged woman in Figure 3.1 will get some rejuvenation. You can work with a photo of yourself, your mom, your wife, or Martha Stewart.

1. Let's start by whitening her teeth. Zoom in on the smile. Choose the Dodge tool at the bottom of the Tools palette. Dodge still shares a room with Burn and Sponge, even though their punk rock band broke up years ago.

2. Dodge has one function. It says "lighten up." Apply the Dodge tool to each tooth using a circular motion. Accept the default Range (Midtones). Adjust Exposure and brush size as needed. Figure 3.2 shows before and after, as well as the work of a crazed dental hygienist.

NOTE

You'll know when you've gone too far. Fortunately, Photoshop has numerous levels of Undo or History states so you can go back in time.

Figure 3.1
Before treatment, but after signing away her right to sue if anything goes wrong. (Photo courtesy of RubberBall.com.)

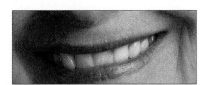
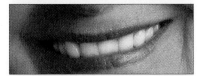
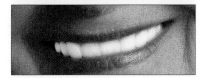

Figure 3.2
Stop before you get to Stepford White.

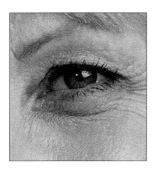

Figure 3.3
Blurry vision.

These images show the effects of a few well-placed strokes with the Spot Healing Brush. With Proximity Match as the Type option, this tool senses that the pixels you drag your stylus or mouse over differ from the surrounding pixels. That difference is corrected seamlessly. For best results, paint short strokes that follow the contour of the crease or other flaw you want to remove.

Worry lines gone.

No mo' crow.

Blurring the lines

We can do quite a bit of "youthing" with the Blur tool. You'll find Blur shares office space with two other attorneys, Sharpen and Smudge.

3. Apply the Blur tool to the crinkly areas of skin above and below the eye, and wherever just a little smoothing will help. Use Normal mode, 100% Strength, and a brush larger than the pupil of her eye but smaller than the iris. Figure 3.3 shows before and after.

NOTE

Blurring can't handle deep creases or crow's feet. The Spot Healing Brush will work wonders on those areas. This is an amazing tool! Its icon is a band-aid with a circular spot. Don't confuse it with its roommate, the Healing Brush (a spotless icon), which acts more like the Clone Stamp tool.

4. Choose the Spot Healing Brush. Paint a stroke over the brow crease above the bridge of the nose. You'll see a marching ants selection in the shape of your stroke for a moment, then the stroke fills in to match the area around it. Work on the crow's feet, one crow toe at a time.

May I Take Your Bags, Ma'am?

Time to handle the bags under her eyes. We'll use the standard Healing Brush for that, which is even more miraculous than the Spot Healing Brush.

5. Switch to the standard Healing Brush. This tool requires that you specify source pixels from somewhere in the image, just like the Clone Stamp. Hold down the Option/Alt key and click near the highlight on her cheek to establish that as the source. Leave the Aligned option off.

6. Paint a stroke or two along the crease under her eye, and watch as the years fall away.

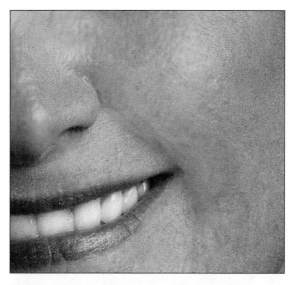

Figure 3.4
Keep smiling or your face could break.

Cheek Repair Time

Let's tackle the slight sagging of her cheek and that little fatty deposit starting to show between the corner of her mouth and the naso-labial fold.

7. Choose the Clone Stamp tool. Hold down the modifier key (Option/Alt) as you click near the highlight of the cheek. Begin painting the shadow under the cheek. Change opacity, brush size, and source pixel as needed. Aligned should be turned off.

    A little practice and experimentation with the Clone Stamp and the Healing Brushes should enable you get the results shown in Figure 3.4.

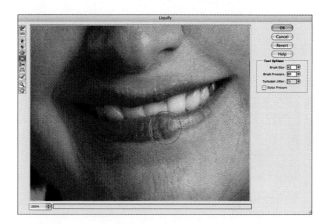

Figure 3.5
Lip service.

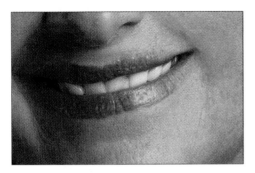

Figure 3.6
As good as a collagen injection.

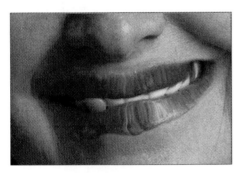

Figure 3.7
Nurse, hand me the Reconstruct tool!

Figure 3.8
Dahling, you look mahvelous! New hairdo?

Finish with the Lips

Plastic surgery is a lot like fine art—it's hard to know when you're finished. Before we let our patient leave the operating room, let's plump up those lips.

8. Choose Filter, Distort, Liquify and zoom in so that the mouth fills the screen. Liquify is like a separate mini-application with its own Tools palette and Brush controls. The usual zoom and scroll controls are available.

9. Find the Bloat tool (great name!) halfway down the toolbar and use a brush size slightly bigger than the width of her lip. Drag slowly across the lip to enlarge it evenly, as shown in Figure 3.5.

    If things don't go too badly, you should get something similar to Figure 3.6.

TIP

When you're working with Liquify things can go horribly wrong in a hurry. See Figure 3.7 for a fairly mild example of what could happen if you're not careful. Fortunately, there is a Reconstruct tool (third from the bottom on the toolbar) that allows you to paint back the original pixels wherever they are needed. Photoshop CS has a few additional Liquify tools and controls, such as the capability to "freeze" pixels to protect them from distortion.

Compare the original face to the youthified (youngered?) version in Figure 3.8.

Project 2: **Fast Forward**

While some of us may want to look younger, others want to look older… old enough to drink, perhaps, or old enough to take advantage of the senior discount at the movies. The man in Figure 3.9 appears to be in his thirties. We can get him a lot closer to Social Security and Medicare overnight.

I. Let's dull that brilliant smile a bit. Choose the Burn tool, which shares space with Dodge and Sponge. (Yes, they have a rock band called The Toners.) It is a darkener, just what we need here. Use a tooth-size brush with the default Range (Midtones) and Exposure (**50%**). Paint across the teeth until they are about as dark as shown in Figure 3.10.

Figure 3.9
Thirty-something. (Photo courtesy of RubberBall.com.)

Figure 3.10
Tall, dark, and dingy.

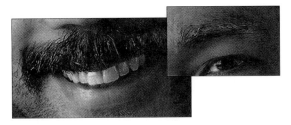

Figure 3.11
Silver threads among the black.

2. Switch to the Dodge tool to give him some gray hairs. We used the Dodge tool to lighten the teeth in the previous project, remember? Paint over the eyebrows and moustache. This time start with the Midtones Range option then switch to Highlights for some additional silvery strokes. You may need to use the Sponge tool to desaturate (remove excess color). Figure 3.11 shows the salt-and-pepper look.

TIP

The mustache and eyebrow on the shadow side are too dark to respond to the Dodge tool as desired. I used the Clone Stamp tool, which enables you to paint pixels from one part of the image to another. Hold down your Option/Alt key and click to establish the source pixels, in this case the mustache and eyebrow on the lighter side of his face. See Chapter two for more cloning tips.

When I applied similar Dodge strokes to the hair on his head the effect didn't look like graying strands. The image shows his hair just looks more shiny and curly. We'll have to try something else: a receding hairline!

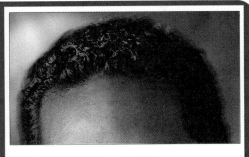

Shiny & Curly. Larry & Moe.

The Backup Plan

Before we attempt anything drastic, we'll need a safety net.

3. Make a new layer that is exactly the same as the image, by dragging the background to the New Layer icon in the Layers palette, as shown in Figure 3.12.

Figure 3.12
Safety features.

NOTE

Photoshop CS users won't need that safety layer. You have the History Brush, which can paint back to any previous state you designate. Now aren't you glad you paid full price and got all the bells and whistles?

TIP

Now we can do all the damage we want to on the background copy. If we want to recover any areas from the original, we can simply use the standard Eraser to reveal the pristine version underneath. It will also be handy to toggle the visibility of the Copy layer on and off to have a quick look at the before-and-after version.

Hair Today…

Ready to lose some hair? There are at least two ways to do it, not counting having kids.

4. Select the forehead and hairline with the Lasso tool, as shown in Figure 3.13. Use Free Transform (Command/Ctrl+T) to pull the top of the bounding box up. If you need to reposition one of the lower corners of the bounding box use the Command/Ctrl key as you pull a corner handle. Figure 3.14 shows the new position of the hairline.

Figure 3.13
Prepare for a forehead-raising.

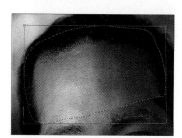

Figure 3.14
Smooth move.

Here's another way to make hair recede. Use the Clone Stamp tool to paint more skin above the hairline. First, establish the source pixels by clicking on the forehead with your Option/Alt key down. Release the modifier key and start painting where you want the new (higher) hairline. Be sure the Aligned option is checked. The challenge is to avoid obvious streaks and repeats, as in this image.

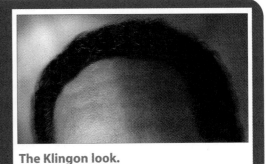

The Klingon look.

TIP

If you prefer to work without those pesky marching ants in the way, Command/Ctrl+H will toggle off their visibility. That "H" stands for "hide."

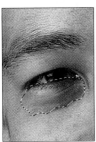  

Figure 3.15
Carry that bag for you, sir?

Exaggerate the Imperfections

Put some puffiness under the eyes by using the Dodge and Burn tools in tandem; Dodge to make highlights and Burn to create shadows. Let any existing creases guide you. You'll just exaggerate them.

5. Use the Lasso tool to make a selection for the bottom edge of the eye bags we'll create, as in the left portion of Figure 3.15. The upper edge of the selection won't matter. Feather the selection by a pixel or two for a subtler effect.

6. Choose the Burn tool. Reduce Exposure to about **30%** and resize the brush as needed. Paint a shadow along the lower edge of the selection.

7. Switch to the Dodge tool and return to the default Range (Midtones). Paint a highlight above the shadow. For a subtle blending of skin tones, deselect and use the Blur tool.

Would You Like Some Brow with that Furrow?

Paint some creases in the forehead with very small Dodge and Burn brushes at low opacity.

8. Choose either Dodge or Burn and the Soft Round 5 pixel brush from the Default brush presets menu, or use the bracket keys to get the size you want. Stick with the Midtones Range, but vary Exposure as needed.

9. Paint over any existing creases to emphasize them, then add a few new ones. Observe the direction of the light source, so that your highlights and shadows maintain a visual logic as you work. Irregular lines will be more convincing than smooth ones.

   See Figure 3.16 for the effect of this technique on a completely different face.

10. That firm jawline will slacken with age. Choose the Clone Stamp tool again. Option/Alt click to establish some chin stubble for your source. Turn the Aligned option off and paint over the hard edge of his chin. Notice the crosshairs moving as you work, showing exactly where the pixels are coming from. Change opacity and source as needed to get the results shown in Figure 3.17.

   Ears get bigger as we age, so I enlarged them using the same select and transform method used for the receding hairline.

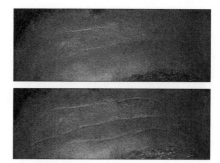

Figure 3.16
Crease increase

Figure 3.17
Older. But wiser?

Project 3: **Who's the Tallest of Them All?**

We've created the illusion of youth and the semblance of aging; now we'll work our magic on the vertically challenged. Unless you're going out for Olympic gymnastics, being tall is a distinct advantage in American culture. Figure 3.18 shows my petite niece, Nesa, with three classmates at their high school prom.

Figure 3.18
Nesa's the short one. (Photo courtesy of Nesa Levy.)

Level with Me

First, let's fix the angle of the image. Whoever took this shot was not holding the camera vertically. Drapes don't hang at a slant like that.

1. Select, All (Command/Ctrl+A) and apply Image, Transform, Free Transform (Command/Ctrl+T). Move the cursor near a corner of the bounding box. When the cursor looks like a curved double-headed arrow rotate the bounding box so the drapes hang perfectly, as in Figure 3.19.

2. Press the Return key to commit the transform. Don't worry about cropping the image until later.

Figure 3.19
Angle fixed, Nesa still short.

Decide which Subjects to Alter

We can either make Nesa taller relative to the other girls in the picture, or make them shorter. Let's make the two girls on the right shorter.

3. Use the Lasso tool (L) to make a selection around the two girls as shown in Figure 3.20. The ideal selection will fit snugly along Armanda's dress (she's wearing the black necklace) and include all the curtains above their bodies. This will minimize the amount of repair work needed later.

4. Edit, Copy (Command/Ctrl +C) and Edit, Paste (Command/Ctrl +V) the selection. Now the two girls are on their own layer. Figure 3.21 shows the Layers palette after the Paste command.

5. Use the Move tool (V) to drag the layer downward until Armanda is about the same height as Nesa. This reveals the tops of their heads on the original backgound, as shown in Figure 3.22. We'll fix that next.

TIP

It's important to keep the layer from shifting right or left as you move it down. A shift would spoil the smooth folds of the curtains. The way to constrain that movement is by holding down the Shift key. Ironic, using Shift to prevent shift.

Figure 3.20
Lasso them gals, yeehah!

Figure 3.21
Layer them gals, wahooo!

Figure 3.22
Black blobs seen floating above heads at senior prom!

Figure 3.23
Helpful hints for clone work.

Figure 3.24
More helpful hints, or colorful graffiti.

6. We'll use the Clone Stamp (S) to cover the tops of the original girls' heads with the curtains. Click on a crease in the curtain while holding down the Option/Alt key to establish the source pixel. I painted a red crosshairs in Figure 3.23 to suggest a good source pixel and a purple spot to show where to begin painting clone strokes. Enable the Align option for the Clone Stamp so each stroke will be offset the proper amount from the source pixel. Also check the Use All Layers box.

NOTE

If you can repair this section of the image in one stroke, it won't matter if you have Align on or off. And you should get extra points for being able to do it in one stroke. I approach Photoshopping (the folks at Adobe hate that word) like a sport, where style counts. You strive for the most elegant, effortless way to accomplish an effect. Finally, a sport that doesn't require you to be in good physical shape. Oh, yeah, I forgot bowling.

Retouch and Touchup

Okay, let's work on the ragged area between Nesa and Armanda.

7. Click on the Background in the Layers palette to make it the target for this step. Clone another piece of curtain over the "old" shoulder showing between the girls' heads.

   Figure 3.24 has color-coded help for the next several steps.

8. Make the layer active and choose the Eraser tool (E). Carefully erase the excess pixels around Armanda's shoulder and dress. Bright green in Figure 3.23 shows where to erase.

9. Merge the layer into the background with the Flatten Image command in the Layers menu.

10. Clone curtain fabric over the original chunk of dress, indicated with yellow in Figure 3.24.

Final Repairs

We'll have to perform a skin graft on Nesa's shoulder to cover the dark blob, shown with a red triangle. Assume that the proper blood tests and compatibility matches have been performed, and Armanda is an appropriate shoulder donor.

11. Use the Lasso tool to select the area of shoulder shown with the dotted red line. Copy and paste to make this a new layer and move it into position on Nesa.

12. Erase excess parts of the skin graft as needed. Reduce the opacity of the layer temporarily so you can see where to erase.

The figure shows our progress at this point. It's reasonably convincing if you don't notice that Nesa's arm would now have to be very, very long to reach Armanda's waist. That's why I circled her hand in Figure 3.24 and added an arrow indicating it needs to be moved up. Frankly, at this point I'm inclined to just clone some curtain and dress fabric over that hand and be done with it.

What long arms you have!

Figure 3.25
Got the red out.

13. Zoom in to see a tiny bit of the dreaded "red-eye" effect in Nesa's right eye. Armanda has it, too. Use the Red Eye Removal tool to fix that problem. You'll find it right under the Cookie Cutter tool, another dandy item that Photoshop CS doesn't offer. Just drag it over the pupil of any offending eye and the red just disappears. See Figure 3.25. Sorry, it won't work on bloodshot eyes.

And here they are, in Figure 3.26, nicely cropped. Three average sized young women and one statuesque amazon. Hey, it's all relative.

Figure 3.26
Heighten your prospects for success in college.

Project 1:
Elastic Surgery

Project 2:
Distort Reform

Project 3:
**A Hair-raising
Experience**

Project 4:
**Oral Surgery Gone
Wrong**

Chapter 4

A Cruel Twist of Face

Wondering how you'd look with a nose job? Don't make any life-altering decisions until you see the outcome in Photoshop. How about a new hairdo or moustache? For even more fun, manipulate the faces of friends, family members, and high-ranking government officials.

Project 1: **Elastic Surgery**

Figure 4.1 shows a familiar face editorialized with Photoshop's Liquify feature.

We'll do one of these together, starting with the beautiful model in Figure 4.2. (Why am I feeling so excited at the prospect of making this woman look really bad? I dunno, but it's cheaper than seeing a therapist.)

1. Open **Asianmodel.jpg**, shown in Figure 4.2.

Figure 4.1
His evil twin?

Figure 4.2
Let's mess this babe up good. (Photo courtesy of ShutterStock.com.)

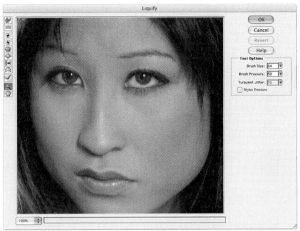

Figure 4.3
About to get gooey.

2. Choose Filter, Distort, Liquify. Figure 4.3 shows the tools and controls available while an image is in the Liquify environment.

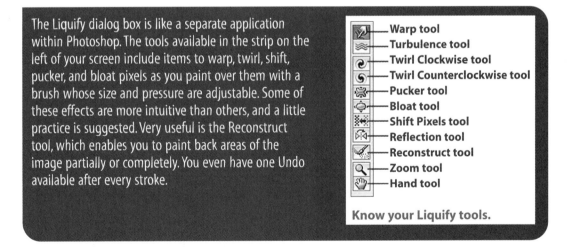

The Liquify dialog box is like a separate application within Photoshop. The tools available in the strip on the left of your screen include items to warp, twirl, shift, pucker, and bloat pixels as you paint over them with a brush whose size and pressure are adjustable. Some of these effects are more intuitive than others, and a little practice is suggested. Very useful is the Reconstruct tool, which enables you to paint back areas of the image partially or completely. You even have one Undo available after every stroke.

—**Warp tool**
—**Turbulence tool**
—**Twirl Clockwise tool**
—**Twirl Counterclockwise tool**
—**Pucker tool**
—**Bloat tool**
—**Shift Pixels tool**
—**Reflection tool**
—**Reconstruct tool**
—**Zoom tool**
—**Hand tool**

Know your Liquify tools.

TIP

Your Liquify strokes will be more predictable if you understand how each of the painting tools in the Liquify palette behaves. A certain amount of trial and error (I like to call it trial and success) is necessary, of course, but some guidelines will help.

Figure 4.4 shows a normal eye with several Liquify effects applied. In the center of the top row, the Pucker tool was dragged horizontally from one corner of the eye to the other. Top right shows the result of using the Bloat tool in a circular motion, increasing the size of the circle slightly as you paint.

The Shift Pixels tool is direction-sensitive. Stroke to the right to shift pixels up, as in the lower-left example. Drag left to shift pixels down, as shown in the center of the bottom row. Not shown here, painting down will shift pixels right; painting up shifts them left. In the last example, notice the effect of gently stroking the inner corner of the eye with the Twirl Clockwise tool, with Twirl Counterclockwise applied to the outer corner.

3. Let's use the Warp tool to mangle the mouth and get her nose out of joint. Warp simply pushes pixels in the direction you drag them. Figure 4.5 shows two of many possible results. I used a brush size around 85px.

4. Use the Pucker tool to make one eye really tiny. Try a back-and-forth stroke horizontally for best results. Apply Pucker to the other eye, but distort it differently. Beauty is often about symmetry, so this will deal a major blow.

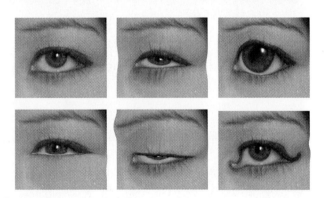

Figure 4.4
Eye chart.

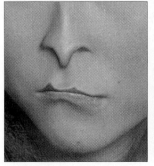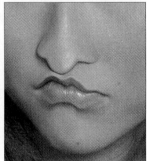

Figure 4.5
A new kind of liposuction?

Figure 4.6
If looks could kill…

5. Switch to the Shift Pixels tool and push an eyebrow around. Use the Reconstruct tool if needed to get something interesting, like Figure 4.6.

Squinty and pinched seem to be favorites of mine, but you can go in other directions. See what I did with the model in the first image. I used the Bloat tool for the eye, Warp and Bloat for the mouth, Shift Pixels to reshape the nose, and Warp strokes to make his hair spiky and his ear pointy. After clicking OK to return to the standard Photoshop tools I repaired the liquefied background. The bloated eye was too flat, so I cloned in the reflection from his other eye.

A fresh victim. (Photo courtesy of ShutterStock.com.)

Pointy and spiky.

Project 2: **Distort Reform**

Several filters in the Distort group provide easier and more predictable ways to achieve effects similar to painting with Liquify tools. Let's play with some of those. Believe it or not, the guy in Figure 4.7 is the "before" version.

1. Open **AverageJoe.jpg**, or any face you want to work with.

2. Choose Filter, Distort, Pinch to see a preview of the effect (similar to Liquify's Pucker tool) using the settings shown in Figure 4.8. The mesh shows exactly how the pixels will be distorted, with maximum pinch in the center of the image. Click on the minus sign check box to zoom out so you can see the whole face. No need to actually apply the effect, unless you must, so click Cancel.

TIP

When you apply a filter without selecting an area of the image, the effect is applied to the entire image. Imagine how much control you can have when you make selections first! Well, you don't have to imagine. You can do it right now.

Figure 4.7
Below-average Joe. (Photo courtesy of Corbis.)

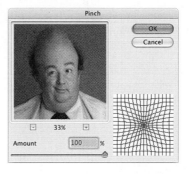

Figure 4.8
Pucker up and Pinch me!

Figure 4.9
Ready for a pinch in the eye?

Figure 4.10
Weirder-than-average Joe.

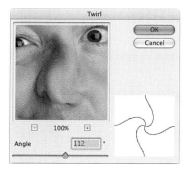

Figure 4.11
The wise-guy effect.

Distort the Eyes

Joe's eyes are already asymmetrical, but I can't resist exaggerating the difference even more.

3. Choose the Elliptical Marquee tool to select his right eye (the squinty one), including upper and lower eyelid, as shown in Figure 4.9.

NOTE

In the following steps all filters used are in the Distort category, so I'll omit the usual path instructions for finding them.

4. Apply the Pinch filter, using 65% on the amount slider, or any amount you prefer.

5. Drag the selection marquee over to the other eye (you can do this with any selection tool active, not the Move tool). Apply the Spherize filter. My settings are 75% for the amount and Vertical Only for Mode.

   Figure 4.10 shows the results of the eye distortions, as well as the nose and mouth effects we will apply in the following steps.

6. Use the Lasso tool to select the nose, including some of the upper lip and cheeks.

7. Apply the Twirl filter just enough to give him a broken nose. Figure 4.11 shows the Twirl dialog box with a preview of the effect.

8. Select the mouth along with some extra flesh around it and apply the Wave filter. Figure 4.12 shows how complex this effect is, with many settings available. Don't let that scare you. (Photoshop Elements can sense your fear. That's a new feature in version 3.) Just fiddle with the sliders and buttons until you get something you like.

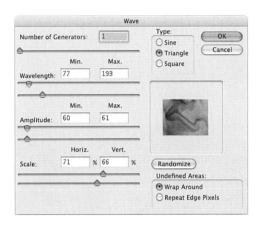

Figure 4.12

Got just one generator, Cap'n, dunno if she can hold!

The series of images seen here is the mouth sampler I created for my favorite distort filters. You might recognize the Wave effect in the upper right. The upper left shows Twirl with an angle of 112 degrees, and the center of the top row has the Spherize effect at 100% in Normal mode (both horizontal and vertical distortion).

Moving to the bottom row, on the left is ZigZag, with its settings shown in the ZigZag dialog box. The center sample is Pinch, and the last item is a Shear effect, with the curve I established shown in the Shear dialog box.

Eeny, meeny, miney mouth.

Shear poetry.

He zigged when he should have zagged.

Project 3: **A Hair-raising Experience**

Changing your hair is a great way to get a dramatic new look, and it's much safer than surgery. Let's take the young man in Figure 4.13 to the salon for a color treatment. No need for rubber gloves.

Figure 4.13
Wondering if blondes really do have more fun.
(Photo courtesy of RubberBall.)

1. Open **Male06.jpg** and choose the Dodge tool. With the Range set for Midtones in the Options bar, paint freely all over the hair with a large brush. Then switch to the Highlights range and paint once again. Figure 4.14 shows the result.

Figure 4.14
Lighten up!

2. Click on the Foreground Color swatch at the bottom of the Tools palette to access the Color Picker. Find a bright golden yellow. Figure 4.15 shows my choice. If you're a stickler for exactitude, enter the actual RGB values and click OK.

3. Choose the Brush tool and select Color Mode in the Options bar. Paint freely all over the hair with a large brush size. Figure 4.16 shows the brassy, artificial look at this point. If that's not a problem for you, you're done.

4. Let's tone down some of the screechy highlights. Switch to the Sponge tool. Use Desaturate mode and a small brush size to make random strokes that follow the direction of locks of hair. Be careful not to let the Sponge touch the skin: grayish bits of flesh are so unattractive.

Figure 4.17 shows streaky and uneven color, and that works for me.

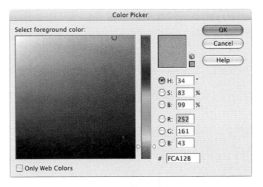

Figure 4.15
Honey, does R252 G161 B43 make me look fat?

Figure 4.16
Gold as brass.

Figure 4.17
Are my roots showing?

Figure 4.18
Just a little off the top.

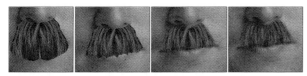

Figure 4.19
Moustache wax and wane.

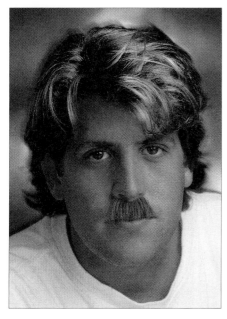

Figure 4.20   **The fruit of our labors.**

Build Your Own Crumb-catcher

All he needs now is a matching moustache, or a contrasting one. Let's build one from his original hair, before it was color-treated.

5. Use Save As to give your working image another name and open the original Male06 file. Make a Lasso selection of hair as shown in Figure 4.18.

6. Use the Move tool to drag-and-drop the swatch of hair to the blonde version of this fellow. Move this new layer into position and rotate the bounding box to the proper angle. He now has half a moustache.

7. You still have the Move tool active. Hold down the Option/Alt key and drag a copy of the layer to the other side of his upper lip.

8. Image, Rotate, Flip Layer Horizontal. Figure 4.19 shows the moustache elements in place, along with stages in trimming and styling from the next steps.

9. Combine the two moustache parts into one layer as follows: Click on the top layer and use the Merge Down command in the Layers menu.

10. Use the Eraser tool to trim the bottom of the moustache, revealing the lower lip. A slightly ragged edge will add realism. Reduce opacity and size of the Eraser tool and carefully work to blend the edges of the moustache into the face.

11. The center of the moustache has hairs growing at odd angles, so let's fix that with the Clone Stamp tool. Option/Alt click to establish source pixels on either side, then paint gently in the center. Repeat cloning as needed to eliminate any obvious repeat patterns.

Figure 4.20 has the finished makeover.

The hairstyles shown here were created without gel or mousse, but with Distort filters.

As a safety net, make a copy of the image by dragging the "background" to the New Layer icon on the Layers palette. This will allow you to erase any unwanted distortion and reveal the original pixels. Select the hair on the layer copy loosely with the Lasso tool. Use the Twirl filter with an angle of −316 to get the effect shown on the left. Use Wave for the curly style on the right, with the settings shown. Changing the layer's blending mode to Lighten did the trick for the Wave effect.

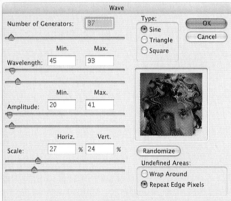

Fabulous!

Project 4: **Oral Surgery Gone Wrong**

One more exercise to show how we can alter an existing moustache and mouth drastically.

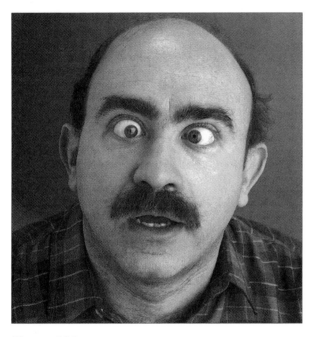

Figure 4.21
What are you doing with that scalpel? (Photo courtesy of Corbis.)

1. Open **crosseyed.jpg**, shown in Figure 4.21.

2. Make an elliptical selection around the mouth and Select, Feather it about 5 pixels, for a softer edge to the effect we will apply next.

3. Choose the Distort, Polar Coordinates filter and designate Polar to Rectangular for the style. Figure 4.22 shows the selection before and after the distortion.

4. With the selection still active, Edit, Copy it to the clipboard.

5. Undo the Polar Coordinates effect or use Edit, Revert to Saved.

6. Edit, Paste the distorted mouth to automatically make a new layer. Move the layer downward to make enough room below the nose for the original moustache.

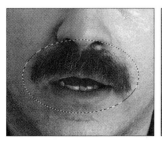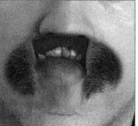

Figure 4.22
"Hghtn Mffln!" ("Help me!")

7. Carefully erase the upper part of the
   layer to reveal the original moustache.
   See Figure 4.23 for the terrifying result:
   mutton chop whiskers and serious
   malocclusion.

You've heard of tummy tucks, but not
too many people go in for mouth tucks.
It's a simple procedure done with the
Pinch filter, set to 73% in this case.
Consider it as an alternative to drastic
gastric surgery for weight loss. It's just
so hard to get food into such a tiny
mouth.

Figure 4.23
Singer in a barbershop quartet.

Smallmouth or wall-eye?

Project 1:
Warts and All

Project 2:
Pock Marks the Spot

Project 3:
Gratuitous Violence

Project 4:
Collision Coverage

Chapter 5

From Insult to Injury

Photoshop has some powerful tools for removing and repairing imperfections. How boring is that? It's way more fun to start with perfection and then mess it up. Use Photoshop's retouching capabilities to inflict damage on that special someone without violating the restraining order. Blisters, pockmarks, bruises, and scars are just a few mouse-clicks away.

Project 1: **Warts and All**

The lovely woman in Figure 5.1 looks worried. Maybe she knows she's about to have some skin problems. We'll start with a simple pimple.

1. Open the **Worrywart.jpg** file, or any image you prefer. Make an elliptical selection near the tip of her nose, as shown in Figure 5.2.

2. Using the Eyedropper tool, click on the highlight of her nose to establish the foreground color. Option/Alt click on the side of her nose to get a darker background color.

3. Choose the Gradient tool with the Foreground to Background preset and the Radial style. Figure 5.2 shows the current colors and Gradient options. Drag a gradient diagonally from the upper left edge of the selection to the lower right edge.

TIP

The pimple looks a little flat, so we'll add some shading. But first, hide the visibility of the selection (Command/Ctrl+H) so you can see what you're doing without those pesky marching ants getting in the way.

Figure 5.1
Flawless skin, for now. (Photo courtesy of ShutterStock.)

Figure 5.2 **Where's the Exfoliate tool?**

Figure 5.3
The perfect flaw.

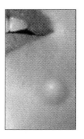

Figure 5.4
The imperfect flaw.

4. Choose the Burn tool. You'll find it at the bottom of the Tools palette, sharing space with the other toning tools, Dodge and Sponge. Reduce brush size to about the diameter of the pimple and gently stroke along the bottom edge of the blemish.

5. Select, Inverse so you can paint a slight shadow under the pimple. Figure 5.3 shows the results, before and after the shading effects.

6. Make another blemish, a bit larger, on her chin or forehead. Feather the selection by two or three pixels before you use the Gradient tool. This will help make the pimple look (ugh!) juicier.

Bring it to a Head

Want to make that blemish ripe and ready to pop? Add the look of pus (yuk!) as follows:

7. Pick a pale greenish-yellow for the foreground color. Choose the Foreground to Transparent Gradient preset (second from the left). Drag from the center of the highlight just a few pixels in any direction.

8. That pimple is too perfect. Deselect it (Command/Ctrl+D) and use the Smudge tool to drag a few strokes from just outside its edge toward the center. A slightly irregular surface looks more convincing, as you can see in Figure 5.4.

Add a Lip Blemish

We're just getting warmed up. Let's put a fever blister (or is it a cold sore?) on her lip. Whatever you call it, it will occupy its own layer.

9. Click on the New Layer icon on the Layers palette.

10. Make an elliptical selection near the bottom of her lower lip. Fill with a radial gradient as before, this time using a foreground color sampled from the lip highlight and a background color sampled from a darker part of the lip. The left side of Figure 5.5 shows this stage.

11. Use Free Transform (Command/Ctrl+T) to rotate the blister to match the angle of the lower lip. The Eraser (at low opacity) and Blur tool are good choices for shaping and blending it into the lip and surrounding skin.

Maybe They Can Freeze That Off...

Now, let's make a wart on her cheek.

12. Create a basic pimple gradient on a separate layer, following steps 1 through 3, but this time use the Lasso tool to make a deliberately irregular selection.

13. Use Filter, Noise, Add Noise to give it a grainy texture. Figure 5.6 shows the recommended settings: Uniform Distribution and Monochromatic. The preview is at 300%, so the blemish looks extremely pixelated.

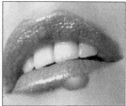

Figure 5.5
Birth of a blister.

Add some irregularity, as you did to the big pimple, to make the blister look more organic. Add a couple of highlights with the Brush tool. Repeat the technique you did earlier using the Smudge tool. This time drag some pixels outward from the blister into the surrounding skin. Reposition, if needed, with the Move tool.

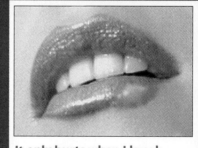

It only hurts when I laugh.

Figure 5.6
Noises on.

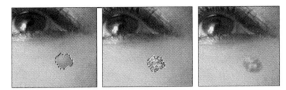

Figure 5.7
Warts new?

14. Apply Filter, Blur, Blur More to the wart.

15. For a rosy glow, sample pink from her lips and paint with the Brush tool in Color mode.

16. Select Invert in order to create a shadow. Use the Brush tool to paint with a color sampled from the shadow under her nostril. Use a brush size slightly smaller than the wart and turn opacity down to about **40%**. Figure 5.7 shows stages of the wart's development.

She's ready for her new career as e "before" model.

TIP

It's easy to add a few more warts here and there. Use the Move tool with the Option/Alt key and drag a copy of the wart to another spot. Change size and reduce opacity for variations.

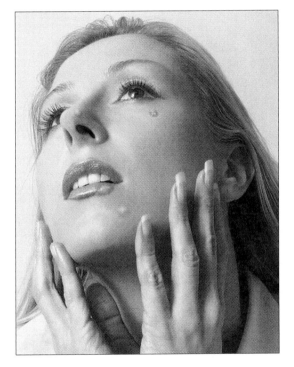

Figure 5.8
Maybe she can pose for a Clearasil ad.

Project 2: **Pock Marks the Spot**

Here's a quick-and-dirty way to give somebody an epidermal nightmare. We'll give this chap some skin with the exact texture of the surface of the moon!

I. Open **Skyman.jpg**, or the portrait you want to work with, and the **moonsurface.jpg** file. Both are shown in Figure 5.9.

Figure 5.9
The face of the moon. (Photo courtesy of ShutterStock.)

Figure 5.10
He must have a dark side.

Figure 5.11
Lunar layer.

2. Use the Move tool to drag and drop the moonsurface image to the face, where it creates a new layer. Use the Rotate and Flip tools on the layer as needed to match the lighting on the face. Change the default Normal blending mode to Soft Light and reduce the opacity of the layer as desired. Figure 5.10 shows the layer moved into place, and you can see the current Layers palette in Figure 5.11.

3. Make a copy of the layer by dragging it to the New Layer icon. Move the layer copy to the forehead. Rotate or flip it to avoid an obvious repeat of the same crater patterns on the other side. Make sure your light source is consistent.

4. Choose the Eraser tool and work with various opacity settings around the edges of the layers to blend them seamlessly into the skin (see Figure 5.12). Use number keys for quick changes in opacity: 3 for 30%, 6 for 60%, and so on.

NOTE

You made a perfect stranger into an imperfect stranger. Have even more fun giving bad skin to a Hollywood personality. For example, you could easily turn Brad Pitt into Brad Pitted.

Figure 5.12
It's the pits.

These variations were created by making a negative of the moon image. Filter, Adjustments, Invert (Command/Ctrl+I) will accomplish that. The first composite uses Overlay mode instead of Soft Light, with layer opacity at 40%. The moon layer in the second image is in Color Burn mode at 25% opacity. As if this poor woman hasn't suffered enough!

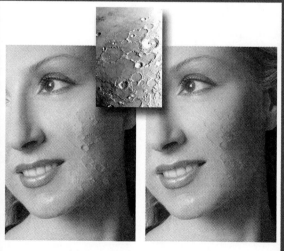

Lunar inversion. (Photo courtesy of ShutterStock.)

Project 3: **Gratuitous Violence**

With a little special effect makeup, the guy in Figure 5.13 will look like he had a fistfight over that hotdog. We'll give him a black eye, a swollen lip, and several abrasions.

Figure 5.13
Lookin' for a fight? (Photo courtesy of Corbis.)

1. Open the **HotdogGuy.jpg** file or another image you want to work with. Make an irregular Lasso selection around his right eye. Subtract the eyeball from the selection by holding down Option/Alt while you drag the Lasso around it. Select, Feather and enter **5** for the pixel radius, to soften the edge of the selection a bit.

TIP

"Black eyes" aren't really black; they're mostly purple and green. So, find a nice sickly green and bruised purple for your colors. If you want to use my colors, enter these values in the color picker: the purple is R98 G75 B129; the green is R103 G133 B108. It doesn't matter which is foreground and which is background.

2. Choose the Gradient tool with the Foreground to Background preset and Multiply Mode in the Options bar. Set Opacity to about **75%**. Pick your choice for style: Linear or Radial work fine.

Figure 5.14 shows the selection before and after the Gradient fill.

3. Deselect the eye (Command/Ctrl +D) and choose Filter, Distort, Liquify for access to a wide range of distortion tools (information on how to use the Liquify tools can be found in Chapter 4, "A Cruel Twist of Face"). Use the Bloat tool to make his lips puffy in a couple of places. Drag the Pucker tool across the blackened eye to close it a bit, and use the Warp tool on the upper lid of his "good" eye. Figure 5.15 shows this poor fellow in the Liquify environment.

4. Make a new layer for some scraped skin. Use the Lasso tool to select a ragged area on his cheek and feather it about 10px.

5. Find a low saturation red in the Color Picker for the foreground color. I'm using **R161 G68 B80**. Choose the Brush tool and load the Faux Finish Brushes, then find the Plastic Wrap-Dark 40 pixels preset. Figure 5.16 shows the Brush presets menu displayed as a large list. Apply the brush in Normal mode at about **50%** opacity with a few clicks or dabs, rather than strokes. This will take advantage of the rough texture.

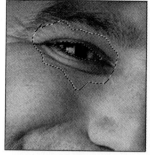

Figure 5.14
Cruisin' for a bruisin'.

Figure 5.15
Puckered and bloated and warped, oh my!

Figure 5.16
I like it rough.

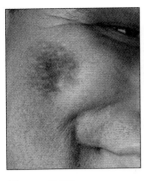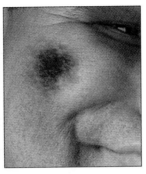

Figure 5.17
You've got bloody cheek!

This image shows the original abrasion, the fresh-looking one on the chin, and five more copies. Can you find them? There's one on his lower lip in Soft Light mode for a pinkish discoloration, and another for the bloody nose, using Overlay mode. My personal favorite is the copy on the bridge of his nose in Difference mode, for the look of an old greenish bruise from a previous altercation. Finally, there are two copies on his knuckles in Darken mode.

You want a knuckle sandwich?

6. Switch to a brighter red and a smaller brush size (20px) to dab darker bloody spots in the center of the selection. Figure 5.17 shows the abrasion developing.

Contuse and Re-use

Once you've got a realistic abrasion on its own layer, you'll be able to use it in several more places on the face, with some lovely variations.

7. Copy the layer and move it to his chin with the Move tool and the Option/Alt key down. Distort its shape by pulling one or more of the handles on the bounding box. With the Command/Ctrl key down you can move a corner handle independent of the others. Try another blending mode, such as Pin Light for the look of fresh bright blood.

8. Save the image in Photoshop format with layers intact.

Project 4: **Collision Coverage**

Let's use some of your hard-fought skills to inflict damage on inanimate objects. The shiny red sports car in Figure 5.18 appears to be due for a wheel imbalance and misalignment.

1. Open **Redcar.jpg**. It's only a '97 Honda, but it will do. Apply some distortions with the Liquify tools. Have some fun with Warp, Bloat, and Shift Pixels. Crush the top, wrinkle the hood, and flatten a tire or two. Try to get something similar to Figure 5.19. (See Chapter 4 for tips on using Liquify effects.)

2. Destroy that nice shiny paint job in the next few steps. First, use the Sponge tool to paint random areas of lower saturation. Sponge shares space on the toolbar with the other toning tools, Dodge and Burn. Choose Desaturate in the Options bar and about **30%** Flow.

3. The Dodge and Burn tools will enable you to shape and enhance the dents. Use a brush size around 40px and the default Range (Midtones). Paint a Dodge stroke on the upper part of a dent to lighten it, and paint a Burn stroke just under that for a shadow.

Figure 5.18
Showroom fresh. (Photo courtesy of ArtExplosion.)

Figure 5.19
Fender bender.

Figure 5.20
Just transportation.

Figure 5.21
Wraparound windshield.

4. The bright highlights of the original will lose their luster when you paint flat red over them with the Brush tool in Darken mode at about **60%** opacity. Figure 5.20 looks like a junker already.

Remove the Windshield

I'm a little worried about that windshield cracking. Let's replace all the glass with plastic sheeting, as shown in Figure 5.21. It's much safer.

5. Use the Magnetic Lasso to select the windshield. The Magnetic Lasso is a good choice when you want to select an irregular shape with defined edges.

6. Apply Filter, Artistic, Plastic Wrap. I used a high amount (**15**) for Highlight Strength, moderate setting (**8**) for Detail, and low amount (**3**) for Smoothness.

7. Select each of the other sections of glass and repeat the Plastic Wrap effect. I used a slightly higher setting for Detail to make more crinkles in the plastic on the side windows.

Make a Leak

I don't know much about cars, except that I need a new one about every 15 years, but shouldn't there be some transmission fluid or anti-freeze or something leaking out of the engine by now? Let's make a puddle of viscous greenish fluid under this wreck.

Figure 5.22
A quart low.

8. Use the Magnetic Lasso again, to make a clean selection along the front edge of the car, then just drag freehand to make a smooth outer edge for the puddle. One nice thing about the Magnetic Lasso is that it acts like the standard Lasso when there are no edges around. Figure 5.22 shows the selection marquee on the left.

9. Find a dark green for the foreground color. Choose the Gradient tool with the Foreground to Transparent preset and the Linear style. Other options: Normal mode and **100%** opacity. Drag the gradient from the lower edge of the selection to the upper edge. The center of Figure 5.22 shows the result.

10. Add some Burn strokes to strengthen the shadow under the car and at the extreme outer edge of the puddle. A few Dodge strokes near the outer edge will give the liquid a three-dimensional look, as seen in the final section of Figure 5.22. Dodge strokes for a car… like, ironic.

11. Just a few more finishing touches. Crack the front reflector by using the Magic Wand to select parts of it and fill it with black. Use the ever-popular Dodge tool to make the vinyl and rubber look weathered.

It's hard to know when you're done with this project. The side view mirrors are still intact, but I'm running on empty. Now take this image to a few body shops and bring three estimates to your insurance company.

Makes me really appreciate my '97 Honda.

Damage the Finish

Remember the abrasions we made on the hotdog guy in the previous project? Sure you do. Did you save the image without flattening the layers? Of course you did. But if you didn't make it or save it, refer to steps 4, 5, and 6 in the "Gratuitous Violence" project to make an abrasion for the car. Just read "paint" for "skin."

12. Open the layered **HotdogGuy** file and drag any one of the abrasion layers to the sports car image. Make two more copies of the abrasion for the car. Resize and position them as shown in the final image. The blending modes I used are Color Burn on the passenger door, Darken on the fender, and Vivid Light on the hood.

Project 1:
Where Am I? An Incredible City

Project 2:
Stonedhenge

Project 3:
Environmental Deception

Chapter 6

Location, Location, Location

If you've been reading this book like a novel, beginning with Chapter 1 and working your way through the chapters consecutively, you've noticed that most of the projects so far have involved images of people. That is about to change. If you haven't been reading this book like a novel, then you haven't noticed the serious flaws in the plot and the scarcity of sympathetic characters to identify with.

Project 1: Where Am I? An Incredible City

Ever wake up in a strange city, wondering where you were? Maybe you shouldn't have had so much vodka the night before. In this exercise you'll create a city that's not just strange, but impossible.

1. I have no idea what city is shown in Figure 6.1. (I don't get around much.) You can work with either **Seattle.jpg** or **Aukland.jpg**. I'll be adding the incompatible collection of famous buildings shown in Figure 6.2 to this skyline. Make your selections from the landmark images on the *Fun with Photoshop Elements 3* website.

Figure 6.1
Name that town! (Photo courtesy of ArtExplosion.)

Figure 6.2
Meanwhile, somewhere in Europe. (Photos courtesy of ArtExplosion.)

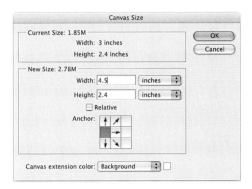

Figure 6.3
There are metric units, too, for you Europeans.

Figure 6.4
More water, more sky! As long as you're up, more wine.

NOTE

Some touching up will be needed to make the new water and sky blend seamlessly with the original, but we can do that after we add more landmarks. As I interpret the "sport" of Photoshop, you get style points for not doing anything unless and until it's necessary. This interpretation is motivated by efficiency and (I admit it) laziness.

Add Some Breathing Room

Let's open up the space we have to play with, extending the image horizontally. We won't distort the existing skyline, just add more pixels.

2. Image, Resize, Canvas Size enables you to add blank pixels in any amount and direction you specify. We'll add 1.5 inches to the right side of the image. Settings are shown in Figure 6.3.

3. Let's fill that empty white space with some sea and sky. Make a rectangular selection of enough water to fill the lower-right corner. Drag it into place using the Move tool with your Option/Alt key down, so you leave the original water in place.

4. Here's how to use the existing sky to fill the remaining white area. Use the Magic Wand at default Tolerance (32px) to select the sky with a single click. Edit, Copy the selection to the clipboard. Now click the Magic Wand in the white space to select it and use Edit, Paste into Selection. Drag the pasted sky to the upper edge of the image. Figure 6.4 shows the image at this point.

5. Deselect (Command/Ctrl+D) and use the Eyedropper to sample the pale blue-green of the sky, below the streaky part. Use the Paint Bucket tool to fill the remaining white space with color.

Drop in a Landmark

Let's put Big Ben into the picture.

6. First, increase Tolerance of the Magic Wand to about 50px to select the sky around the clock tower. Be sure the Contiguous option is checked so you don't pick up bits of blue in the clock face. You'll probably need to make several clicks with the Shift key down until you have most of the sky selected. Use Select, Grow to pick up any stray pixels. Select, Inverse.

7. Use the Move tool to drag and drop Big Ben to the skyline, where it becomes a new layer. Resize and position the layer as needed. Yes, it appears to be floating in the air in Figure 6.5. Don't worry about that yet. We're keeping our options open for a while.

8. Now let's add the Arc de Triomphe, with the same techniques you used for Big Ben. Selecting the sky with the Magic Wand is a snap. Well, a click. Two clicks, really, in order to include the sky inside the arch. Select, Inverse and drag the arch to the composite image with the Move tool.

Compound the Confusion with Another Landmark

I like having the arch dominate this imaginary city, so let's place it offshore, as shown in Figure 6.6. Again, don't worry about cleaning up the excess stuff at the bottom just yet.

Figure 6.5
I say, Ben old boy, be happy she didn't stick you in the water.

Figure 6.6
I see London, I see France.

Figure 6.7
Bring on the urban gladiators!

9. Use the same basic approach to get the coliseum into the picture. This time turn off the Contiguous option for the Magic Wand, so you can include the bits of blue that are not connected to the main sky area. Place this new item as shown in Figure 6.7 (visibility of the arch and clock tower is turned off). You'll need to reduce the size of the layer by dragging a corner of its bounding box. Trim away the excess at the bottom, so that the coliseum is flush with the edge of the water.

So, you've got all the elements on layers. Now have some fun moving and resizing things until you're happy. My arrangement in this image shows the stuff around the bottom of the arch eliminated. I managed to hide the seam between the coliseum and the original skyline, and also avoided having to fix the bottom of the clock tower. Now that's efficient!

Capital City, but what country?

Color Corrections

Let's look carefully at the composite before we flatten the image. The original skyline has a warm, lemony tone. The coliseum is cooler (bluish) in color. We can fix that.

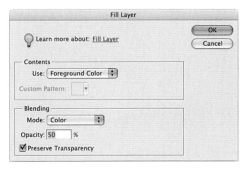

Figure 6.8
After this, you won't look bluish.

10. Use the Eyedropper tool to sample a grayish yellow from one of the background buildings. Make the coliseum the active layer. Choose Edit, Fill Layer, with the settings shown in Figure 6.8. Enable Preserve Transparency to protect the transparent pixels on the layer from the fill.

11. Now it's safe to flatten the image. You'll find that command in the More menu on the Layers palette.

12. The sky still has some weird building-shaped areas left over from steps 4 and 5. Use the Clone Stamp to touch up the sky (and the water, if needed). Option/Alt click will establish source pixels from a "clean" area. Release the modifier key and paint over the problem pixels. (Refer to projects 2 and 3 in Chapter 2 for tips on cloning techniques.)

Figure 6.9
No reflection? Must be the Arch of the Vampire!

Boost the Realism

We've come so far, I'd hate to let a tiny detail spoil the effect. Can you find it in Figure 6.9? There should be a reflection of the arch in the water!

13. Make a rectangular selection on either base of the arch. The height of the selection needs to be about the distance from the bottom of the arch to the bottom of the image. Use the Shift key to add the same size selection on the other base. Copy and Paste to put these two rectangles on a new layer.

Figure 6.10
It's Tuesday, but this can't be Belgium.

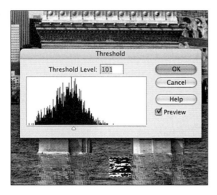

Figure 6.11
Pixels to the left of the arrow are black; those to the right are white.

Figure 6.12
Custom brush can paint with water.

14. Image, Rotate, Flip Layer Vertical and move the mirror image layer into position below the arch. Reduce opacity to about **50%**.

15. Apply Filter, Distort, Ripple, with the amount slider set at maximum and Small in the size field. Figure 6.10 shows the reflection layer before and after distortion.

Ripples Complete the Effect

If you're really picky, you'll notice the ripples of the reflection don't quite match the ripples on the rest of the water. Fix that in the next steps by making a new brush based on the brightness values of the water.

16. With the background layer active, select a small square area of the water between the two bases of the arch. Use Filter, Adjustments, Threshold to convert the selection to high-contrast black and white. Figure 6.11 shows the effect along with my Threshold setting.

17. Edit, Define Brush from Selection brings up the dialog box shown in Figure 6.12. Name the new brush and click OK. Your "water" brush will be added to the current Brush presets. Undo the Threshold command to restore the blue water.

18. Choose the Eraser tool and use the new brush at about **50%** opacity to dab several times on the reflection layer. You might need to increase the opacity of the layer. Figure 6.13 shows a more convincing reflection. You can decide if it was worth the extra work.

Figure 6.13
On reflection, I think it was worth the trouble.

Project 2: Stonedhenge

Let's create another location, not from city landmarks this time, but from ancient stones. You'll need several samples of graffiti for this project. You can acquire them by doing an image search on Google.com (see Appendix A, "Resources," for help). Take a peek at the sidebar to see the graffiti bits I'm using.

Figure 6.14
Everybody must get stones. (Photos courtesy of ShutterStock.)

1. Open **StonehengeA.jpg** and **StonehengeB.jpg**, two views of the same awesome ruins in England, shown in Figure 6.14. We'll splice them together just to make the composition more interesting.

2. Select the sky in **StonehengeB** with the Magic Wand, using Tolerance set to about 12 and Contiguous turned off. Select, Invert and drag the stones and grass to the **StonehengeA** image with the Move tool, placing it as shown in Figure 6.15.

Figure 6.15
Looks like a postcard

Stonehenge is no longer open to public access for fear of vandalism. We can get around that. I found samples of graffiti from all over the world on the Internet. You can Google up the items shown here or create your own.

Graffiti for recycling.

3. Drag and drop your graffiti to the Stonehenge composite. Resize, rotate, and erase as needed. Change the blending mode and opacity to make a variety of combinations. Figure 6.16 has nine pieces of graffiti in place. Blending modes used were: Multiply, Darken, Lighten, Difference, Pin Light, Hard Light, Color Burn and Overlay.

4. Save in Photoshop format to keep all the layers intact, in case you want to make changes later. Then flatten it and Save As a JPEG or TIFF image.

NOTE

I made those Stonehenge images post-card size for a reason. You can place text on your finished piece, using techniques in Chapter 8, "The Write Stuff."

Figure 6.16
Virtual vandalism.

Project 3: **Environmental Deception**

Prepare to spend some quality time putting incompatible environments together. Why? Because we can. Figures 6.17 and 6.18 show how easy it can be to make a saltwater forest.

Figure 6.17
Turf and surf. (Photos courtesy of ShutterStock and Nesa Levy.)

I. Open **bigtrees.jpg**. and **beach1.jpg** and select the sand and water (everything except the sky) with the Polygon Lasso tool. Use the Move tool to drag and drop your selection to the **bigtrees** image.

2. Use the Eraser at about 30% opacity to make the upper edge of the beach layer slightly transparent and irregular, so it will blend with the forest and reveal a little of the trees below the surface of the water.

Figure 6.18
Can't see the ocean for the trees.

If you thought that was quick and easy, just put these two images together. Open sunset2.jpg and winterwoods.jpg. Drag and drop either image to the other one. Change blending mode to Lighten and the sunset becomes a golden globe speeding through the woods, leaving a trail of smoke. There's even a reflection in the puddle.

Water and woods again, but different. (Photos courtesy of Nesa Levy.)

UFO sighting?

Create "Head for the Hills" Weather Conditions

Those two combinations were just appetizers. Here's the main course. Figure 6.19 shows a winter scene with a couple of cars on the road. The other source image features a wavy sea. We'll give the drivers of those cars a much more exciting trip.

Figure 6.19   **More woods, more water.** (Photos courtesy of BigFoto and ShutterStock.)

Figure 6.20
So it's not perfect. We're just here for fun.

I. Open **oceanwaves.jpg**. We need to select the waves in the foreground. The Lasso is too crude a tool for managing such detailed edges. The Background Eraser will be helpful. It shares a space with the standard Eraser tool and has a tiny scissors icon. Figure 6.20 shows a detail of the image after I used the Background Eraser along the upper edge of the waves. After that "path" was made, it was easy to use the Lasso tool to surround and delete the upper part of the image.

NOTE

The Background Eraser works best when there is high contrast at the edges, such as the rocks in this image. There are settings for fine-tuning the sensitivity of the tool, and it's important to drag the hot spot (crosshair) exactly on the color you want to erase.

TIP

You can quickly become a power user of any version of Photoshop by learning the ins and outs of selection. Use the Magic Wand when selecting based on color and value. Use the Lasso when selecting a freehand or polygon shape, the Magnetic version for irregular shapes with contrasting edges. Complex selections can be made and refined using any of the selection tools in combination. Add to an existing selection with the Shift key down; subtract pixels with the Option/Alt key down. Use the Feather command for a soft edge, and the Invert command to select what was unselected and vice versa. Save selections for loading later. Those are the basics. Now practice, practice, practice.

2. Open **WinterRoad.jpg**. Drag-and-drop the ocean waves selection to the winter scene, where it creates its own layer. Figure 6.21 shows the wave layer in place.

3. Reduce opacity of the water layer to about **70%**, enough to see the cars. Choose the standard Eraser tool and erase a little at a time, until the cars are floating at the level you want. Not too high in the water; it's not the Dead Sea (the snow is a clue). Figure 6.22 shows stages in revealing the cars. Be sure to create ragged edges to the water lapping up around the cars.

4. Save the version you like, but keep working on some variations. Simply switch blending modes for unexpected and dramatic effects in an instant. Figure 6.23 shows the layer in Normal mode and a detail using Luminosity mode. The water got gray and the car's tail-lights are glowing through it. Cool!

Figure 6.21
Dude! Where are my cars?

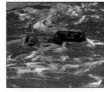 

Figure 6.22
Coming up for air

Figure 6.23
I think the engine's flooded!

This variation includes the snowbanks and the edge of the road, with a big wave just about to crash over our unlucky travelers. It looks like it took a lot of work, but It was completely unplanned. Another lucky blending accident, this time thanks to Lighten mode.

The second image shows the illusion is spoiled where snow on the trees shows through the waves. In Lighten mode lighter pixels "win" so all I had to do was darken the bottom (dry) layer. A little sloppy painting with black did the trick.

We are really, really lost!

Okay, honey, next time we'll take that cruise.

Honey, is there a black hole on the map?

Project 1:
**A Room for
Improvement**

Project 2:
**Cabinet
Appointments**

Project 3:
**A Realtor's
Nightmare**

Project 4:
**Housepainter's
Fantasy**

Chapter 7

Just Faux Fun

Whether your room could use new wallpaper or your whole house needs a makeover, this is the chapter for you. Do some virtual interior or exterior decorating. If you like the results, hire a contractor to make the changes final (and undoable). You might even discover you have a flair for surface design and launch a new career.

Project 1: **A Room for Improvement**

The interior shown in Figure 7.1 is a bit too bland for my taste. I'd like to see that wall with the picture on it covered with the elegant abstract fabric.

1. Open the image you want to work with. You'll find some choices on the Fun with Photoshop website, or do a Google image search for "staircase." You won't need this exact staircase to do these (um) steps.

Work the Wall

The wall is a complex shape, composed mostly of line segments and with a single curve. We'll need to use a combination of techniques to select it.

2. Choose the Polygon Lasso and click on the corners of the wall shape. This selects most of the wall, including the framed print and the potted plant. All that's left out is the little piece behind the curved banister. Figure 7.2 shows the selection filled with purple so you can easily see its boundaries. I just like purple.

3. Add the curved shape to the selection by holding the Shift key down while you click with the Magic Wand tool. Use the default Tolerance (32) for the Magic Wand. Select, Save Selection and name it **wall** or something equally obvious. You can load the selection anytime. For now, deselect it.

Figure 7.1
Simple elegance. (Photo courtesy of ArtExplosion.)

Figure 7.2
Purple passage.

The series of three images shows the stages in this maneuver. It can be hard to tell exactly what is and isn't selected with all those marching ants running around, so hide the visibility of the selection (Command/Ctrl+H) and do a quick fill or delete (which you will undo) to see a solid color as in the final image. Delete/Backspace fills with the background color (white by default) and Option/Alt+Delete/Backspace fills with the foreground color.

Leaves and stems.

I really do like purple.

4. Select the potted plant. Two or three Magic Wand clicks with the Shift key down and Contiguous enabled will get most of it. Zoom in to 200% so you can see your work better.

5. Here's a clever way to include those thin leaves and stems into your selection. Switch to the Lasso tool, and hold the Shift key down to add the area of wall surrounding the stems. Choose the Magic Wand again to subtract the wall pixels. The Option/Alt modifier key must be used for subtracting. Tweak the selection until you're satisfied, then save the selection as **plant** or whatever.

6. Make a copy of the background by dragging it to the New Layer icon on the Layers palette, as shown in Figure 7.3. Do your work on the Background copy, leaving the original image as a safety net in case you want to retrieve parts of it later.

7. Open the **Fabric.jpg** image. Select, All, followed by Edit, Copy to place it on the clipboard.

8. Return to the staircase image and load the wall selection with the Select, Load Selection command. Use Edit, Paste into Selection. Use the Move tool to enlarge the fabric to fill the wall. Choose Image, Transform, Perspective and drag one of the corner handles on the right edge of the bounding box to match the angle of the fabric to the angle of the wall. See Figure 7.4.

9. Bring the potted plant back by loading its selection and using the Delete/ Backspace key on the fabric layer.

10. The wall looks too flat in the section at the right, which is in shadow. Switch to Multiply blending mode to fix that.

> **NOTE**
>
> Multiply mode allows the warm creamy color from the background to come through. I like that. It also lets the framed print come through, and I don't like that. We're going to hide it with something much better. I found a Matisse drawing that's absolutely fabulous for this room.

Figure 7.3
Play it safe. Avoid design injuries.

Figure 7.4
Gettin' busy as a one-armed paper-hanger.

Figure 7.5
Potted plant, $20. Wall fabric, $200. Matisse drawing… priceless.

> **TIP**
>
> Selecting the stairs is a challenge that can be handled in a variety of ways. There are defined edges, so the Magnetic Lasso should be considered. There are several straight edges, so the Polygon Lasso seems an attractive choice. There is value contrast with the surrounding areas, so the Magic Wand can work. I'm guessing I can rely on the Magic Wand and accomplish the task in the fewest clicks. That's less work, more style points, and (most important of all) longer coffee breaks.

11. Use the Move tool to drag and drop the Matisse nude, or any artwork you wish, onto the composite. Image, Transform, Perspective will help you enhance the illusion. Figure 7.5 shows the drawing in place.

12. Put a cheap frame around this artwork that sold for more than two million dollars at auction. Use Edit, Stroke (Outline) Selection with Black about 5 pixels wide.

13. Let's give the stair carpet a color sampled from the new wall. Use the Eyedropper tool to click on a plum or mauve shade. If you don't know what colors those are, you probably shouldn't be working on an interior decorating project, not without supervision.

14. Choose the Magic Wand tool with Contiguous turned on and Tolerance set to **40** pixels. Click on the dark upper stairs and add to the selection by Shift-clicking two more times or until most of the upper staircase is selected. Reduce Tolerance to the default **32** before you Shift-click on the lower stairs.

Clean the Stairs

I got the selection shown in Figure 7.6 with six clicks of the Magic Wand tool. There are still some thin strips of bright pixels on the top stairs that weren't picked up by the Magic Wand.

15. A cool way to include a scatter of unselected pixels is with Select, Modify, Smooth. Specify about **6** pixels for the Sample Radius. Or you could drag a Lasso around the stray pixels. Be sure to use the Shift key when adding pixels. And it wouldn't hurt to save the selection.

16. Ready to change the color of the stair carpet? Use Edit, Fill Selection, with Foreground Color for the Contents, Color for the Blending Mode and **100%** Opacity.

Don't Forget the Molding

Oops! Some of those triangular bits on the molding above the stairs got colored, too. Don't worry, as long as you have the original "safety net" background layer.

17. Use the Eraser tool to reveal the original creamy color in those triangular areas. Figure 7.7 shows the new carpet color and the erasures in progress, along with the Layers palette.

Figure 7.6
Fourteen stairs in six clicks. Can you beat that?

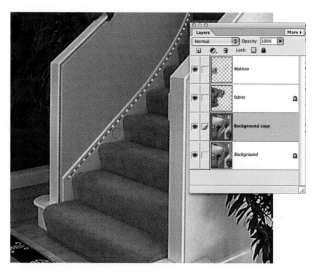

Figure 7.7
Staircase to Heaven.

Figure 7.8
Is the marble Venus too much?

Brighten the Wall

One final touch before moving on. I'd like to brighten up that fabric wall a bit.

18. Load the wall selection, so you can restrict an adjustment layer to that area. Create a Brightness/Contrast Adjustment Layer, using **+32** for the Brightness setting and **+18** for Contrast.

    Figure 7.8 shows the final redecorating job. I couldn't resist adding a statue. This is an exciting improvement on the boring interior we started with!

Now let's move on to the kitchen. We've earned a snack. We'll also have another adventure in surface design.

Project 2: **Cabinet Appointments**

The kitchen in Figure 7.9 looks so sterile it could be in a hospital. There's no indication of what could be inside those cabinets. Drugs? Bandages? Specimen cups?

We will apply custom patterns to the doors of each cabinet. Figure 7.10 gives you a taste of what's in store. Coffee beans and pasta decorate two of the cabinets. Let's make food patterns.

Figure 7.9
Sterile environment. (Photo courtesy of ArtExplosion.)

Figure 7.10
Two basic food groups.

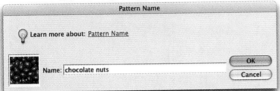

Figure 7.11
Chock full o' nuts. (Photo courtesy of ArtExplosion.)

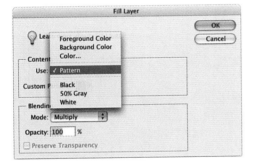

Figure 7.12
Fillings, nothing more than fillings.

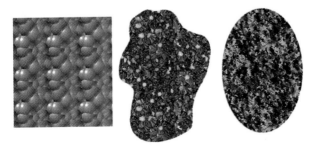

Figure 7.13
Bubbles, Purple Daisies, and Stucco.

1. Open **coffeebeans.jpg**. I'm using chocolate covered nuts, from the same basic food group: brown. Make a large rectangular selection, similar to the one in Figure 7.11.

2. Edit, Define Pattern from Selection brings up a dialog box for naming a new pattern, also shown in Figure 7.12. When you click OK, it becomes part of the current pattern collection.

TIP

Photoshop offers several sets of patterns that can be used to fill selections. Edit, Fill Selection brings up the dialog box in Figure 7.12. A pattern is a seamless repeat of a single rectangular image "tile." Figure 7.13 shows three pattern fills. From left to right they are from the Default Patterns, Nature Patterns, and one of the Texture Fill pattern collections. It's easy to see the repeat in the Bubbles pattern. Any unfeathered rectangular selection can be made into a custom pattern repeat, but it might take some work to create the seamless effect. None of Photoshop's pattern presets contain food imagery. I've been meaning to talk to Adobe about that.

3. Use File, New (Command/Ctrl+N) to make a blank RGB document big enough to test your new pattern. A three-inch square at 300ppi is fine. Edit, Fill Selection is now Edit, Fill Layer, because there is no selection. Choose "chocolate nuts" from the Pattern picker and Normal blending mode at **100%** opacity. You can see the edges of the tile in Figure 7.14, but the effect is acceptable.

4. Choose the Polygon Lasso tool and select one of the cabinet doors. Edit, Fill Selection with the pattern. Figure 7.15 has the results.

Make a Seamless Pattern

I think the pattern is too big, and there's no way to resize it. We'll have to create a smaller version from scratch. And we might as well make it really seamless this time.

5. Do you still have that test image from step 3? If not, make another one. Use Image, Resize, Image Size to reduce the dimensions by half.

6. Zoom in to see detail clearly and find a repeat that is not at the edges of the tile. Select it so that the same point is at each corner of the rectangle. The left side of Figure 7.16 shows my selection. In the next step we'll get rid of the obvious edges that are inside the selection.

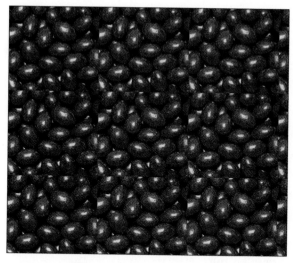

Figure 7.14
Testing, testing.

Figure 7.15
Just one is a whole meal.

Figure 7.16
I've got you cornered.

7. Choose the Clone Stamp tool and use Option/Alt-click to establish source pixels from anywhere in the image. Paint with Aligned option on or off, as you prefer, until the telltale edges are eliminated. The right half of Figure 7.16 shows my finished work.

8. Repeat step 2 to make this a new pattern preset. Give it a unique name, like "small chocolate nuts" because Photoshop won't notice if you use the same names over again. Now repeat step 4 to decorate that kitchen cabinet door.

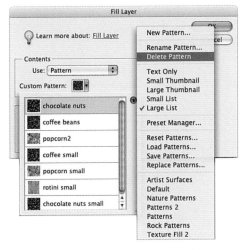

Figure 7.17
Go, nuts!

TIP

You can remove the earlier version or any unwanted patterns with the Delete Pattern command in the Pattern preset pop-up menu, shown in Figure 7.17. Notice the menu options for displaying, loading, and saving pattern groups. I saved all the food patterns I created in this project as FoodGroups.pat, and it's available for download from the Fun with Photoshop Elements 3 website.

I added popcorn, mixed nuts, walnuts, and elbow macaroni to my kitchen décor, pretty much completing the theme of snacks and comfort food. I started leaning toward bigger and bolder pattern fills. I even went back to the original size for the chocolate covered nuts, as you can see in the image. That color scheme of warm browns and yellows works nicely, too. You can't go wrong if you base your design (and your diet) on the three "Cs": chocolate, cheese, and caffeine.

A color-balanced diet.

Project 3: **Realtor's Nightmare**

Nothing makes a worse first impression on potential homebuyers than a bad external paint job. I hope your artistic license is still in effect, because you're about to have your painting contractor's license revoked.

Figure 7.18 shows the two images we can use to turn a house from fresh to flaky in a flash.

I. Open **framehouse.jpg**, or a similar image you prefer. Make a selection of the main wall with the Polygon Lasso. You'll need to subtract the windows and those odd bits under the roof from your selection. Do that with the Option/Alt key held down. Figure 7.19 shows the wall selected. Save the selection for later and deselect it for the next step. (see Appendix B, "Photoshop in a Peanut Shell," for tips on selection techniques.)

Figure 7.18
Basic brown and peeling. (Photos courtesy of ShutterStock.)

Figure 7.19
No munching termites, but plenty of marching ants.

Figure 7.20
Rough housing.

Figure 7.21
A real fixer-upper

2. Open **flakypaint.jpg** and use the Move tool to drag it to the house, where it becomes a new layer. The angle of the paint needs to match the angle of the house, more or less. Change blending mode in the layers palette from Normal to Multiply so you can see the house as you manipulate the layer by dragging the handles of its bounding box. You can rotate by dragging a corner handle when the cursor is a curved double-headed arrow. Figure 7.20 shows the streaks in the paint layer lined up with the edges of the boards on the wall, and slightly enlarged to cover it completely.

3. Prepare to trim the paint. Select, Load Selection and check Inverse in the dialog box. Press Delete/Backspace and the excess paint disappears! Multiply mode is working nicely, too, as seen in Figure 7.21.

Here are some other blending mode variations to consider. I switched to Pin Light for the bright but very crumbly paint on the left. Linear Burn, in the other image, makes it seem like pieces of the wall have actually rotted away.

Blended flakes.

Project 4: **Housepainter's Fantasy**

Here's a quick way to lower property values for the whole neighborhood. Take the stately, matronly mansion in Figure 7.22 and turn her into a hippy crashpad with splashes of shocking Day-Glo paint.

1. Open **mansion.jpg**, similar to the image I'm using. Grab the Paint Bucket tool and change the blending mode from Normal to Overlay. Yes, painting tools have the same menu of blending modes you've been using to combine layers. And as long as you're in the Options bar, be sure Contiguous is checked and reduce Tolerance to about **12**. This will restrict your fills to small irregular areas. Choose a bright, saturated color and start clicking here and there on the stone facade. Switch to other rowdy colors at will and change opacity of the paint bucket just for more variety. For quick color changes open Color Swatches from the Window menu. See Figure 7.23 for inspiration.

Figure 7.22
I'm old, I'm dull, and I'm expensive. (Photo courtesy of ArtExplosion.)

NOTE

Another cool thing about the Paint Bucket options is you can choose to fill with a pattern instead of the foreground color. When you switch to the Pattern fill option, the presets menu shows up so you can pick a pattern from the current group or load another collection. I wanted to revert to the default patterns and was prompted to save my food group patterns (from the previous project).

Figure 7.23
I'm old, I'm stoned, and I miss the sixties.

Figure 7.24
Electric Kool-Aid acid roof.

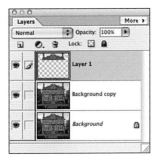

Figure 7.25
Prepare to Merge.

2. Increase Tolerance so you can fill larger areas. Load the default Pattern presets and choose Tie Dye. (Use list display, as shown way back in Figure 7.17, to see names of the patterns.) Click on the roof. Switch to Optical Checkerboard and click on the chimneys and those crenelated shapes (I had to look that up).

3. Switch to the Brush tool, using Overlay mode, and paint the remaining bits of the roof with red and purple or colors sampled from the Tie Dye pattern.

Recover without a Safety Net

That roof looks so groovy it makes me want to redo the splotchy parts. I hadn't followed my own earlier advice, however, and didn't have the pristine image as a safety net. The next steps address that situation.

4. Use the Save As command to give the working image another name. Open the original **graymansion** file again. This time, duplicate the image as a layer so you can work on it with the untouched original waiting underneath to break your fall.

5. Hold the Shift key down and use the Move tool to drag the painted version to your new layered image. Use the Rectangular Marquee to select everything below the psychedelic roof and delete it. The Merge Down command will combine the painted roof with the background copy. You're good to go, again.

Figure 7.24 shows the amazing roof effects and Figure 7.25 has the Layers palette just before the Merge Down command.

Add a Gradient Fill

This time let's give the whole building (except the roof) a colorful gradient fill.

6. Use the Polygon Lasso to click on the four corners of the facade to select it. Choose the Radial Gradient tool with Overlay blending mode at **100%** opacity. Load Color Harmonies 2 and select the Red, Purple, Blue preset or any of the other exciting combinations shown in Figure 7.27. Drag your gradient from the top of the doorway to a corner of the selection.

7. Repeat the technique from step 2, using the Paint Bucket in Overlay mode to fill some of the windows with the Optical Checkerboard at about **50%** opacity. Default Tolerance of **32** should work fine. Figure 7.27 shows the finished mansion, ready to be occupied by the Marquis Facade.

Figure 7.26
What would Color Disharmonies look like?

Here's a cool paint job created with a gradient collection called Noise Samples. I used Blues for a radial effect on the roof and Noisy Spectrum with the linear style on the rest of the house. All the windows were filled with the Molecular pattern from the default pattern presets, using Overlay blending mode at 100%.

Noisy neighbors.

Figure 7.27
Amazing Technicolor Dream House.

Project 1:
Postcard from Somewhere

Project 2:
What Is Mona Lisa Thinking?

Project 3:
Fake Highway Signs

Project 4:
Take It and Stick It! (On Your Bumper)

Chapter 8

The Write Stuff

This chapter is devoted to wordplay. We'll use Photoshop's versatile Type tool to create fake highway signs and slogans for bumper stickers. We'll add dialog balloons to photos for humorous or editorial commentary. Even if you don't know your font from your typeface and you think Auto Kerning was a German general during the big war, you'll learn to make lettering twist and shout.

Project 1: **Postcard from Somewhere**

Figure 8.1 shows the fictitious city we created in Chapter 6, "Location, Location, Location," cropped to the proportions of a standard 6"×4" postcard. If you haven't already pieced this composite together, or if you forgot to save it, not to worry.

1. Open the file called **whatcity.jpg**, available for download from the *Fun with Photoshop Elements 3* website.

2. Choose the Type tool and click anywhere on the image. Type **Having a Wonderful Time. Where Am I?** or something similar. The text will probably appear in black and set in the default font, Helvetica, at a small point size.

3. Drag the Type tool over the text to highlight it, then choose any font, point size, and color you want. Switch to the Move tool to reposition, resize, or rotate the text.

Figure 8.1
Somewhere in Europe, maybe? (Photo courtesy of ArtExplosion.)

Text automatically occupies its own special layer, indicated with a "T" as shown in this image. As long as that big "T" remains, you can edit the text just as if you were using a word-processing program. Change the font, color, alignment, leading, and so on in the Options bar. When you choose Layer, Simplify Layer, the text becomes an ordinary image layer, just pixels. The technical term for this is *rasterizing*, and that's what it's called in Photoshop CS.

Don't rasterize me yet!

Figure 8.2
Whoever dies with the most fonts wins.

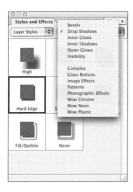

Figure 8.3
Check out Wow Neon. Seriously.

Figure 8.4
Wish you were where?

Tinker with Type

Figure 8.2 shows a couple of possibilities I'm considering. That font on top is Papyrus, using a blue sampled from the water. Copperplate is the typeface used at the bottom, with a Hard Edge Drop Shadow added.

4. Apply a Drop Shadow or another layer style if desired. You'll find a pop-up menu of layer styles in the Styles and Effects palette (see Figure 8.3). To remove a layer style choose Layer, Layer Style, Clear Layer Style.

Postcard Art

I decided on 18pt Techno, set in two lines with center alignment and slightly rotated. See Figure 8.4 for my postcard art ready to flatten, save, and print on glossy photo stock.

Project 2: What Is Mona Lisa Thinking?

DaVinci's Mona Lisa is probably the single most famous image in the entire history of art. Her face has been defaced, used, and abused by practically everybody since Marcel Duchamp painted a mustache on her. She's entitled to be in a bad mood.

1. Open **MonaLisa.jpg**, available for download from the *Fun with Photoshop Elements 3* website. Give her an unpleasant expression with Filter, Distort, Liquify. (See Chapter 4, "A Cruel Twist of Face," for tips.) Or just open the **MonaGrumpy.jpg** file.

2. Create some text to express what she is feeling, using an appropriate type-face. I used a romantic-looking script called Vivaldi in Figure 8.5.

   Consider alternative comments, such as **I'm so sick of you freakin' tourists!**. I'm sure you can come up with something.

Figure 8.5
"I'm not in the mood!"

This image shows the default custom shape picker open and the word balloon shape selected. You can load all 500+ shapes by choosing All Elements from the pop-up menu.

Keeping in shape.

Create a Text Balloon

In the next few steps we'll make a word balloon for the text.

3. Create a new layer. Make sure it is positioned under the text layer. Fill it with white. You'll see only the text on a solid white background.

4. Choose the Cookie Cutter tool. This dandy device, located just under the Crop tool, lets you crop a layer to fit a shape. Click on "Talk 1" in the custom shape picker, then click and drag on the white layer. Everything outside the word balloon will disappear, revealing Mona. Scale and reposition the white shape until you're satisfied, and then click Return. You can still make changes to the shape later, using the Move tool.

Add Special Effects

Figure 8.6 has the word balloon in place. Let's add some special effects on that layer.

5. Choose the Radial Gradient, with the Foreground to Background preset in Normal mode at **100%** opacity. Sample a golden yellow from Mona's forehead with the Eyedropper. Switch foreground and background colors (X), so that white is the foreground color. Lock transparency for the layer to restrict your effect to the white shape (highlight the tiny checkerboard icon on the Layers palette). Whew! That's a lot of preparation. Finally, drag a gradient from the center of the word balloon to slightly outside it.

Figure 8.6
"You got a problem with that?"

Figure 8.7 shows the gradient fill with transparent pixels unaffected. I changed the contents of the type layer just to see if you're paying attention.

6. Choose Layer Styles in the Styles and Effects palette, then open the Bevels library and apply the Simple Inner style. Open the Outer Glows library and apply the Simple style.

TIP

A tiny lowercase "f" (as in *f/x*) inside a black circle will appear in the layer list when you apply a layer style. Double-click on that little icon to have access to some limited controls, such as size and direction. Photoshop CS users will have considerably more controls over every conceivable variable, plus individual visibility controls for each effect on the Layers palette. You can be glad you spent the extra $$ for this feature alone!

7. Reduce opacity of the layer to about **75%** for a translucent parchment look. Flatten the image and you're done. Figure 8.8 shows my finished word balloon with a Simple Inner Bevel and a Simple Outer Glow.

Figure 8.7
"I haven't had a facial in 500 years!"

Figure 8.8
"Maybe later, if you order a pizza."

Project 3: **Fake Highway Signs**

Make a phony invitation to a fictitious birthday party at a nonexistent location using unreasonable directions (like you sometimes get from Mapquest). We'll re-create it, personalized for your own birthday.

Figure 8.9
What's your sign? (Photos courtesy of ArtExplosion.)

1. Open all three source images: **nextright.jpg**, **California1.jpg**, and **Stop.jpg**. **Nextright** will serve as the background for our composite.

2. Use the Magic Wand to select the light background on the California highway sign and Select, Inverse. Drag and drop the sign to the "Next right" image, where it becomes Layer 1. Resize and position it with the Move tool.

Add Perspective

The California 1 North sign looks like it's
either floating in air or sticking in the ground
far away, making it huge. We'll fix that next.

Figure 8.10
**Equally confusing to Californians and
Washingtonians.**

3. Erase the little stump of post on the
   California sign. Use the Rectangular
   Marquee to select one of the posts
   holding up the SeaTac Mall sign. Edit,
   Copy (Cmd/Ctrl+C) and Edit, Paste
   (Cmd/Ctrl+V) so it becomes Layer 2,
   then move it into position. Highlight
   Layer 1 in the Layers palette and choose
   Merge Down in the More menu. Now
   the sign and the post are collapsed into
   one layer, shown in Figure 8.10.

4. Use the Eyedropper tool to sample the
   green on the California sign, then paint
   over all the lettering with the Brush tool.

5. Choose the Type tool and type **TRUTH**
   using Blue Highway D Type or another
   font if you prefer. Drag over the text to
   highlight it for color and size changes.
   Click on the Color swatch in the Options
   bar and sample the light gray from the
   NEXT RIGHT lettering on the background. Change the point size of the
   type in the Options bar if needed. Switch
   to the Move tool to rotate the text
   slightly to align with the green rectangle.

6. Use the Type tool to click on the shield-
   shaped portion of the sign, making a
   new text layer. Type your age at your
   next birthday in a larger point size.

7. Click again for another text layer and
   type your first name plus apostrophe
   "s." How will you get this text on a
   curve? Click on the Create Warped Text
   icon, near the extreme right on the
   Options bar. Use the Arc style with the
   settings shown in Figure 8.11. The
   Bend amount you need will depend on
   the length of your name.

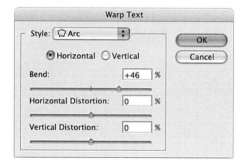

Figure 8.11
Warp it. Warp it good.

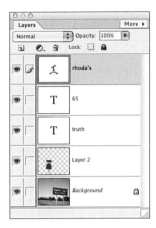

Figure 8.12
Merging traffic ahead.

This image shows a road sign for a fictitious attraction at an imaginary theme park for teenage girls. The back row of lipsticks has brightness and contrast reduced, using an adjustment layer.

Watch out for exfoliation. (Photo courtesy of ArtExplosion.)

8. Your Layers palette should look something like Figure 8.12 at this point. Notice the curved text layer has the Warped Text icon. When you're happy with your new sign turn off visibility of the background and choose Merge Visible from the More menu. Your text will be rasterized automatically. Make the background layer visible again, and highlight it for the next step.

Give Me a Sign

Let's work on the original NEXT RIGHT sign. We'll eliminate the SeaTac Mall text and give the whole sign a fresh coat of paint before we add more type.

9. But first, get rid of those green corners sticking out from the sign's white border. Use the Brush tool to paint over them with a blue sampled from the sky at each corner. You can access the Eyedropper by holding down the Option/Alt key.

10. Use the Magic Wand to select the sign's green background. Sample the green from the sign formerly known as "California1" and use Option/Alt plus Delete/Backspace to fill the selection with this nice fresh green. Paint over the SeaTac text with green.

11. Change foreground color to the pale gray of the sign lettering and use the Type tool to create "(your name here)'s House," using upper- and lowercase instead of all caps.

12. Now for the STOP sign. Click on each corner of the octagon with the Polygon Lasso tool. Drag and drop it to the composite with the Move tool. Resize it and give it a slight perspective tilt with Image, Transform, Distort. Add a new post, as you did in step 3.

13. Make yet another text layer for "DON'T" and "NOW!" You can set both words on the same layer by clicking Return a couple of extra times to get the right spacing. Use Layer, Simplify Layer to rasterize this text, then use Free Transform to match the perspective angle of "STOP."

14. Add one more text layer, using a contrasting font, to give directions to your house. The final invitation is shown in Figure 8.13.

Figure 8.13
I won't really be 65 for many, many... months!

> **NOTE**
> For some really outrageous freeway directions check out www.jillsjokeline.com/hiwaysigns.html.

Project 4: **Take It and Stick It! (On Your Bumper)**

You can rely on text alone (no images) to make your point pointedly with the standard bumper sticker format. Add a simple graphic to enhance the message. Those I Love _____ stickers, using a heart shape for the word "love," can be made with Photoshop's Cookie Cutter tool.

I   my Honda

Figure 8.14
Dude! I blanked my car!

> **TIP**
> Point sizes in the Options bar only go as high as 72, but you can type any number in the size field, or use the Move tool to scale the text, in proportion or not.

Figure 8.15
Too bad there's no more room on my bumper.

1. Use File, New to specify the dimensions and resolution for a blank RGB document. About 11″ × 3″ at 72ppi ought to do it.

2. I chose a font called Techno for a tribute to my car. Figure 8.14 shows this bold condensed typeface at about 140pt, with space for the heart. Use any font you like and type something similar for your car.

3. Make a new layer and fill it with bright red or any color you want for the heart. Drag the color layer under the text layer, so you can see the type.

4. Choose the Cookie Cutter tool. Highlight the heart in the default Custom Shape picker. Click and drag on the image. Adjust size and proportions with the handles on the bounding box, then press Return.

5. Flatten the image, save it, and print on precut self-stick paper. Spray with a coat of waterproof varnish to keep the ink from running and hope that your car will not be affected. See Figure 8.15 for my finished piece.

Bumper Snicker

Let's do one based on the I brake for
_____ category. Browsing the Cookie
Cutter shapes I noticed some paws, and a
sticker saying "I paws for coffee" naturally
came to mind.

Figure 8.16
The paws that refresh.

1. This time I filled the 11″ × 3″ background with brown.

2. I created a new layer, filled it with black,
   and chose Paw Print 2 from the Animal
   Shapes picker. To get the second paw, I
   just made a copy of the layer by dragging it to the new layer icon on the
   Layers palette. See Figure 8.16.

Figure 8.17
Anyplace but Starbucks.

3. Saved the text for last. If you want the
   text to be in white, as I do, switch background and foreground colors (X). Type
   I_____ for coffee, which will be in the
   most recent font used. Change to
   another typeface if you want to. I'm
   using P22 Stanyan Bold. That's the
   same typeface used in the bogus directions to my birthday party, returning to
   the coffee theme.

4. Add a Noisy Drop Shadow to the text
   layer, for the final effect in Figure 8.17.

It might be interesting to fill that solid background with the coffee bean pattern we made in
Chapter 7, "Just Faux Fun." If you weren't around
for that, you'll need to download the FoodGroups
pattern presets from the *Fun with Photoshop
Elements 3* website.

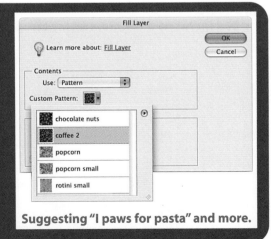

Suggesting "I paws for pasta" and more.

Figure 8.18
Do you want a refill?

5. Highlight the background in the Layers palette. Choose Edit, Fill. In the Fill Layer dialog box use Pattern for the contents. This makes the pattern picker available. It has another menu, where you will choose Replace Patterns and navigate to wherever you saved **FoodGroups.pat**. When that loads choose the coffee bean pattern.

6. Now there's a problem. The black paws don't contrast enough with the patterned background. You can fill the paws layer with white, after making sure you have locked transparency. Or apply the Layer Style shown in Figure 8.18. I chose Small Noisy Border from the Outer Glows effects.

Project 1:
Quick Cartoons

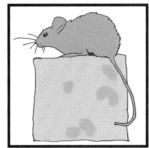

Project 2:
Trace and Fill

Project 3:
Play with Your Food!

Project 4:
Chocolate Treats

Project 5:
Decorate Your Room

Chapter 9

Kid Stuff

When I was a kid, we didn't have computer graphics programs. Heck, we didn't have computers. Cameras were around, using film, but no color film! Those were the Dark Ages... well, the Black and White Ages. Image manipulation was done only by professionals. But I digress.

Anyhoo, this chapter will help you spend some quality time with your kids or just act really immature all by yourself. Here are some indoor activities for kids and grownups to share.

Project 1: **Quick Cartoons**

Let's make the cartoon in Figure 9.1. There's no drawing involved, in case you were worried. You'll use the Cookie Cutter tool to make the colored shapes, then add special effects.

1. Use File, New (Cmd/Ctrl+N) to make a blank file about 9" × 6" at 72ppi resolution in RGB mode with a white background.

NOTE

There are six separate parts to this image, each created on a colored layer. Open the Layers palette if it's not visible. You'll find it listed with all other palettes in the Window menu.

Figure 9.1
Two pets and their people.

2. Click on the New Layer icon six times (and say "there's no place like home"). Your image will have six fresh white layers (and you'll be back in Kansas).

3. Choose the Paint Bucket tool and a bright red foreground color. Click anywhere on the image and the current layer will fill with red. Highlight another layer and click again, so you have two red layers. Use yellow, brown, purple, and blue to fill each of the remaining layers. Figure 9.2 shows your Layers palette at this point. The order of your colors doesn't matter.

Figure 9.2
Red alert and yellow alert I understand, but purple alert?

Figure 9.3
Put on a happy face.

Figure 9.4
I see red people!

4. Switch to the Cookie Cutter tool. It has a heart-shaped icon and is just below the Crop tool. Click to open the Custom Shape picker on the Options bar. Find "Face" in the pop-up menu to get the shapes shown in Figure 9.3 and choose the happy face (face 9 in the list display).

5. Click and drag on one of the red layers. Turn off the visibility of other layers if needed to see the result. Is your face red? It should be.

TIP

To cancel a Cookie Cutter action, press the Escape key. To commit to it, press Return/Enter. If you try to switch to another tool before hitting the Return/Enter key, a dialog box appears asking whether you want to cut the shape or not. You can reposition or resize a shape at any time with the Move tool.

6. Use face 7, the one with the scrunched-up eyes, on your other red layer. See Figure 9.4 for the results at this stage. My background is yellow because that's the color of the next layer in the stack.

7. Load the Animals 2 shapes to get the dog and cat. Create those cutouts on the brown and yellow layers, respectively.

8. Find the goofy glasses for the purple layer and the spiky hair for the blue layer in the Dressup shapes. Make those cutouts. Reposition your shapes with the Move tool.

TIP
You might need to reorder some of your layers to get the hair and glasses on top of the faces and the dog in front of the boy. Just drag them up or down in the Layers palette.

9. Use the Eraser tool to get rid of the girl's original eyes and the boy's excess hair.

Add Special Effects

Yes, you could have done this in a fraction of the time with half a dozen 69-cent felt markers. But, wait, we've got some special effects coming!

10. Open the Styles and Effects palette and choose Patterns from the Layer Styles. Highlight Waves and apply it to the spiky hair layer. There it is in Figure 9.5, near the bottom of the list.

11. Switch to Bevels (at the top of the Layer Effects list) and apply Inner Ridge to the glasses.

12. Drag the cat layer so that it's just under the dog layer, if necessary. Now highlight the dog layer and choose Merge Down from the More menu. This puts both animals on one layer. Let's hope they can get along. Apply the Simple Inner Bevel.

13. Double-click on the "f" icon for the dog-and-cat layer to get access to style settings. Increase Bevel Size to get a puffier effect. Does your finished work look like Figure 9.6?

Figure 9.5
Scroll up for Abstract Fire, Satin Sheets, and … oh, wait, this is the kids' section!

Figure 9.6
Try THIS with felt markers!

This Cookie Cutter landscape was made by filling the layers with patterns instead of solid colors. A section of the Paint Bucket tool Options bar shows the Nature patterns library loaded. I cut one tree shape from a layer filled with the Grass pattern and a different tree shape for the Leaves pattern fill. The Clouds and Tie Dye patterns are in the Default presets. The desert and sky background was made with the Chrome preset for the Gradient tool.

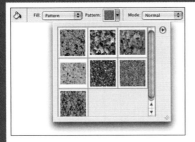

How do you tie dye a butterfly?

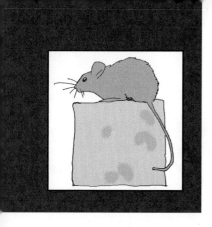

Project 2: **Trace and Fill**

We're going to make a drawing of a rat with some cheese, shown in Figure 9.7. You'll do much better and have more fun if you work with a Wacom tablet and stylus. Ask Mom or Dad to get one for you right away. Nagging and whining are useful techniques, or promise to clean your room. If that doesn't work, I guess you'll have to draw the rat with a mouse.

1. Open the **rat.cheese.jpg** file, available for download from the *Fun with Photoshop Elements 3* website, or use any photo of simple objects.

2. Make a new layer and fill it with white. Turn Opacity of the layer down to about **75%**, so you can see the source image while you work.

3. Choose the Brush tool and pick Soft Round 5 pixels from the Default Brush presets in the Options bar. Use black for the foreground color.

4. Trace the rat and cheese, using simple lines on the outer edges of the forms. Do the rat's eye, but ignore the holes in the cheese. Make some whiskers with single strokes of different lengths. My effort is shown in Figure 9.8.

5. Turn opacity up to **100%** and examine your line work for gaps. Repair any spaces with the Brush.

6. Choose the Paint Bucket with foreground color for the fill source. Change the foreground color to light gray. Make sure your drawing is the target layer, and fill the rat shape with a click.

7. Turn the visibility of the drawing off. Then press your Option/Alt key to have access to the eyedropper function and sample the cheese (yummy!) in the background photo. Make the drawing layer visible again, and highlight it. Click on the cheese area to fill it with color. Don't forget that little bit of cheese above the tail.

Figure 9.7
The rat takes the cheese. (Photo courtesy of ArtExplosion.)

Figure 9.8
DO try this at home.

Does your finished art look much like this image? You've used several hundred dollars' worth of software and hardware to create something that could have been done the old-fashioned way for a couple of bucks. Not a moment too soon! Kids today need to learn how to draw digitally, 'cause analog art supplies are becoming endangered species.

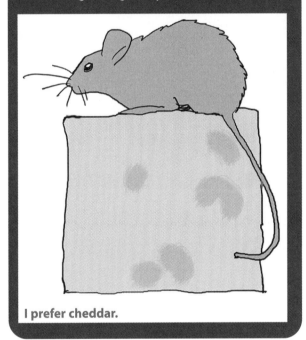

I prefer cheddar.

Is It Cheese Yet?

That yellow block doesn't look much like Swiss or any other cheese, yet. Let's add some of those holes.

8. Switch to the Brush tool again, this time using the Spatter 59 preset. Sample a darker yellow from one of the cheese holes in the photo. Make a few dabs and curved strokes where the holes should be.

Project 3: **Play with Your Food!**

Here's an idea for a contest: Make the most disgusting lunch imaginable. Anything involving raw fish or cooked beets works for me, but we'll do a reptile sandwich.

1. Open **sloppyjoe1.jpg** and **reptile1.jpg**, shown in Figure 9.9.

2. Remove the green background around the lizard by selecting it with the Magic Wand tool and deleting it. Use default Tolerance and the Contiguous option. You'll need to Shift-click to add the pixels between his legs to your selection. The Magnetic Lasso is a good tool for selecting (then deleting) the branch and the two legs on the critter's left side, as shown in Figure 9.10.

3. Select the completely white background with the Magic Wand and Inverse the selection. Use the Move tool to drag-and-drop the lizard to the sandwich, where it will make its own layer.

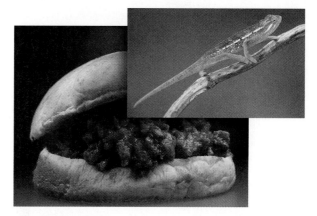

Figure 9.9
For Fear Factor snackers. (Photos courtesy of ShutterStock.)

Figure 9.10
Trim the lizard.

Figure 9.11
Reptilt.

4. Rotate the lizard by dragging on a corner handle of the bounding box when you see the cursor turn into a curved double-headed arrow. Figure 9.11 shows the little guy in position.

5. Switch blending mode in the Layers palette from Normal to Pin Light and lunch is waiting, in Figure 9.12.

In this version, I used another view of the sandwich, sloppyjoe2.jpg. I added a Soft Edge Drop Shadow to the lizard. You'll find it in the Layer Styles category on the Styles and Effects palette. I used the Eraser tool to eliminate the bits of lizard that would be under the bun.

Do you want flies with that?

Figure 9.12
Tastes just like chicken.

Create a Side Dish

How about a side dish to go with our burger?

6. Open **baked.potato.jpg**, shown in Figure 9.13.

Tator Tops?

The melting butter is nice, but we'll need more toppings. Chives? Bacon bits? I know—BUGS!

7. Open **3bugs.jpg**, similar to those shown in Figure 9.14.

8. Drag a rectangular selection around any one of the bugs. I'm using the one on the right. Use Edit, Define Brush from Selection to capture the bug as a new brush tip. You'll name it in the dialog box shown in Figure 9.15.

Figure 9.13
Needs some crunchy bits on top. (Photo courtesy of ArtExplosion.)

Figure 9.14
Potato bugs? Not yet, but soon. (Photo courtesy of ArtExplosion.)

Figure 9.15
Name that brush!

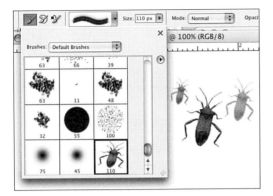

Figure 9.16
Am I bugging you?

9. Choose the Brush tool. Find your new bug brush at the bottom of the brush presets list. Figure 9.16 has the list open, displayed as large thumbnails, along with three marks I made with the brush in different colors and sizes.

10. Make a new layer on the baked potato for your bug topping. Click wherever you want to add a bug. To add lots of bugs with a single stroke, increase Spacing and Scatter in More Options.

You don't have to create a whole series of bug brush presets in different sizes. Use the brush size slider in the Options bar for a quick size change. Even quicker is pressing the left bracket key ([) to get smaller or the right bracket key (]) to get bigger (not you, the brush).

Settings to control brush dynamics are available in the More Options panel shown here. Spacing refers to the amount of overlap in brush "dabs" as you make a stroke. Hue Jitter is handy when you want to create variation between foreground and background color within a single stroke. Increase Scatter to spread the individual dabs around the path of your stroke. Angle is useful unless your brush is perfectly round. Look at Tablet Options, nearby, to enable or disable various Wacom tablet functions.

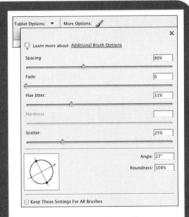

You can make a jitterbug, but not a litterbug.

TIP

Try using black for the foreground color, red for the background color, and increase Hue Jitter to get some color variation. Change the angle setting a few times. Here's another way to create lots of variety: After you have several bugs on the layer, make a copy of the layer by dragging it to the New Layer icon and apply Free Transform (Cmd/Ctrl+T) to change the size and angle of the new layer. All those tricks were used to make the tempting dish in Figure 9.17.

Figure 9.17
Lunch with crunch.

Project 4: **Chocolate Treats**

You need to get the taste of that last project out of your mouth. I know I do. Something made of chocolate should do the trick.

Remember the Cookie Cutter tool we used way back at the beginning of this chapter? We'll use it again to carve some chocolate shapes.

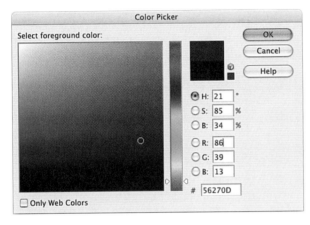

Figure 9.18
R86 G39 B13 looks delicious.

Figure 9.19
A valentine, an Easter Bunny, and some chocolate droppings.

1. Make a new blank RGB file about 8" wide and 4" high, or large enough to fill your screen and give you plenty of room to work.

2. Create three new layers, as you did way back in the first project, and use the Paint Bucket to fill them with rich chocolate color. I suggest milk chocolate for two of the layers, semisweet for the third.

Choose Colors from the Color Picker

The Color Picker in Figure 9.18 shows my current choice. You can type in the RGB values, or just eyeball it.

3. Choose the Cookie Cutter tool. Load All Elements Shapes so you have the entire collection available to you.

4. Find the rabbit in the group of solid animal shapes. Click and drag on one of your chocolate layers. Use a heart shape on another layer.

5. For the third layer use one of the Cookie Cutter splash shapes (Crop Shape 39) to make what will become a spill of hot fudge sauce, I hope. Figure 9.19 shows our three items at this stage.

6. Now we'll apply some layer styles to create the illusion of depth. Use Bevels, as we did with the cartoon shapes earlier. The figure in the sidebar on the following page has Inner Ridge applied to the heart and Simple Inner to the rabbit.

Make a Splash

Making the splash look like a puddle of thick chocolate sauce will be a little trickier. Here's my solution.

7. Make a copy of the splash layer. Leave the copy in place (perfectly covering the original splash) and switch to Hard Light in the blending mode list on the Layers palette. The shape gets a bit darker, but nothing special happens until the next step.

8. Apply the Wow-Chrome Reflecting style to the original splash. Not bad, huh?

Chat in Chocolate

We'll go from splashing chocolate sauce to writing with chocolate frosting. Use the same basic trick from step 7 and 8, but apply it to lettering.

9. Open a new blank white RGB file, about 8" wide by 5" high.

10. Choose the Type tool and type **You're Sweet**, or whatever you want. Change the font to something fun. A typeface with irregular shapes or playful bits is best. I'm using Sand in Figure 9.20. I used the Shiny Edge variation from the Wow Chrome styles. (See Chapter 8, "The Write Stuff," and Appendix B, "Photoshop in a Peanut Shell," for type tips. Appendix A has font resources.)

Here we have the finished heart and rabbit, looking melt-in-your-mouth yummy. Also shown are the splash shape with the Wow Chrome effect alone (see step 8) and the combination of both layer style and blending mode.

Either that's fudge sauce or the rabbit needs more fiber.

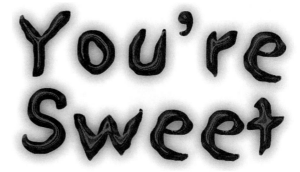

Figure 9.20
Virtual chocolate for low-carb sweetness.

Your choice of Chrome style may vary depending on the specific typeface used, or according to your (um) taste. I don't like the drop shadow that comes built in with the Wow Chrome styles. Thanks to Doug, my tech editor, I just found out how to get rid of it. Double-click the little "f" icon on the layer to access the Style Settings controls shown in this image. Increase the Shadow Distance to the maximum and watch the shadow move completely out of the picture!

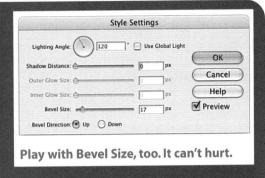

Play with Bevel Size, too. It can't hurt.

Figure 9.21
If you're diabetic, better take more insulin.

Choose a Flavor

Do you prefer a flavor other than chocolate to write with? Well, if you insist, here's how you can make strawberry, or cherry, or lemon.

11. You still have the Text tool active, right? Target the top text layer (the one in color) and drag over the letters to highlight them, or just double-click the "T" thumbnail for the layer. Click on the color swatch in the Options bar. Find a red you like (or yellow for lemon, green for lime… you get the idea).

12. Bright fruit colors will look much better with a change of blending mode from Hard Light to Lighten. Figure 9.21 has red writing. I also changed the font. This one is called "Kids."

Project 5: **Decorate Your Room**

Being sent to your room for misbehavior won't seem so bad if you have the place set up just the way you want it. Warning signs on the door, crime scene tape to keep intruders at a distance, that kinda thing. How about designing your own wallpaper, like the pattern shown in Figure 9.22? Did you have a feeling we weren't quite finished working with bugs?

1. Open **ladybugs.jpg** and **caterpillar1.jpg**, similar to what is shown in Figure 9.23. You'll also need those three bugs from the potato project again, later.

2. Remove the background from the caterpillar image. It's easy with the Magic Eraser. This amazing tool acts like a combination of Magic Wand and Eraser. Just click on a pixel and all pixels of a similar color and value will disappear. You can adjust Tolerance to change the range of colors that are erased. If there are no colors in common between the background and the object turn the Contiguous option off. Clear that background away with just a few clicks!

3. Use Free Transform (Cmd/Ctrl+T) to reduce the caterpillar to half its size. Enable Rulers in the View menu (Cmd/Ctrl+R) to help you find the halfway mark. Hold the Shift key down to prevent distortion as you drag a corner handle of the bounding box.

Figure 9.22   **How do you like my new crawlpaper?**

Figure 9.23   **Let's hope they can share the environment.** (Photos courtesy of ArtExplosion.)

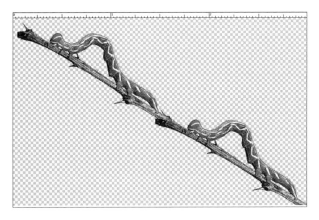

Figure 9.24   **Are you following me?**

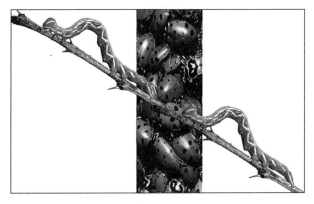

Figure 9.25   **I could swear I saw them moving.**

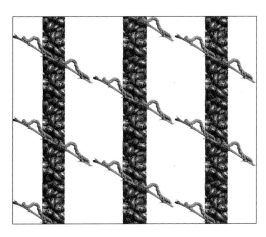

Figure 9.26   **How many pixels per inchworm?**

4. Use the Move tool while holding down Option/Alt to drag a copy of the caterpillar into position, as shown in Figure 9.24. That checkerboard background indicates transparency.

5. Select a vertical strip of ladybugs with the Rectangular Marquee tool and drag it to the caterpillar image. Place this new layer at the bottom of the stack. Stretch it to fit the vertical dimensions if you need to.

6. Flatten the image, and the transparent checkerboard is filled with white. Crop if you have to in order to get the tips of the caterpillar at diagonal corners of the image, as shown in Figure 9.25.

7. You're ready to make this image into a repeating pattern. The current size is fine if you really do use it for wallpaper, but let's work much smaller just for convenience. Use Image, Resize, Image Size to make this file about 4 inches wide at 72ppi.

8. Select, All and choose Define Pattern from Selection in the Edit menu. You'll be prompted to name your pattern, then it becomes available in the current presets.

9. Let's test the pattern. Open a new blank RGB file about 10 inches wide and 6 inches high at 72ppi, big enough so the pattern can repeat a couple of times. Use Edit, Fill Layer and choose Pattern for Contents in the dialog box. Find your new pattern at the bottom of the list in the Custom Pattern picker. Be sure Blending Mode is Normal at **100%** opacity. Your pattern fill should look something like Figure 9.26.

10. Time to bring back those three bugs we used before. They will help decorate the white spaces in the pattern. Copy and paste (or drag and drop) the big bug to one of the white spaces. Put the two smaller bugs in a space in the next vertical column. See Figure 9.27.

11. Repeat step 8 and test your new pattern. Compare it with the sample at the beginning of this project.

NOTE

Figure 9.27 also shows a rectangular selection for making a new pattern that will include the three bugs. That selection was made carefully, to have the same point from the previous pattern at each of the four corners. Notice the caterpillar's nose is used as reference. It was also necessary to find a repeating tile that would not slice through the three bugs.

Figure 9.27
The white shapes are parallelograms, by the way.

For something a little less creepy and much more feminine, try using the lipstick.jpg file shown in the first image for your pattern repeat.

Image, Resize, Canvas Size will let you add some white space to your image. In the Canvas Size dialog box, enter an amount in the Height field that is about double the current height. Anchor the image at the bottom so that all the new white space will appear at the top. Click OK. Select and drag a copy of the lipsticks to the blank area with your Option/Alt key down. Use Image, Rotate, Flip Selection Vertical to get the results in the second image.

Select All and Image, Rotate Selection 90 degrees in either direction to prepare a pattern with vertical stripes. Repeat step 8 and do a test fill on a new 72ppi document about 8" wide by 6" high. Mine is shown in the final image.

I enjoy being a girl. (Photo courtesy of ShutterStock.)

No bugs in the white space this time.

High-tech cosmetics, perhaps?

Project 1:
Not-so-soft Drink

Project 2:
Bugs for Breakfast?

Chapter 10

Fool Me Twice

Combine type with images for fake products. Make labels to print on sticky paper and apply to cans, bottles, and boxes. Surprises galore await unsuspecting visitors to your kitchen cupboard, fridge, or medicine cabinet. Prepare to engage in satire, political incorrectness, and advanced tomfoolery!!

Project 1: **Not-so-soft Drink**

Alcoa invented the pull-ring tab for beverage cans in 1962. Coca-Cola Company introduced a diet soda called Tab in 1963. Coincidence? I think not. It's about time somebody made the connection. We'll create the graphics for a phony product called Tabs.

1. Open the **pulltabs.jpg** and **blank.can.jpg** files, similar to those shown in Figure 10.1.

2. Drag and drop the pull-tabs image to the can, where it becomes a separate layer. Reduce opacity of the layer to about **60%** so you can see the can while you work.

NOTE

Before you begin, install the Blue Highway typeface, available as a free download from Larabie Fonts. You'll have to quit Photoshop Elements and launch it again to have access to new fonts. If you've already created the fake highway signs in Chapter 8, "The Write Stuff," you should be good to go. Or you could get by with another bold sans serif font such as Verdana. See Appendix B, "Photoshop in a Peanut Shell," for type tips and Appendix A, "Resources," for font resources.

Figure 10.1
I drink, therefore I can. (Photo courtesy of ArtExplosion.)

Figure 10.2
The pull-tabs image now covers the surface of the can.

Figure 10.3
The excess pull-tabs imagery has now been trimmed.

3. Use Image, Rotate, Layer 90 degrees Right (Left is okay, too). Choose the Move tool and pull one or more handles of the bounding box so that the pull-tabs image covers the entire cylindrical surface of the can. Use the Shift key to prevent distortion. See Figure 10.2 for this stage.

4. Let's trim away the excess pull-tab pixels. Switch from Normal to Darken in the blending modes list in the Layers palette. That's an easy way to make most of the excess pull-tabs disappear. You'll still have to eliminate unwanted pixels at the top edge of the layer. Make an elliptical selection, as shown in Figure 10.3, and delete.

5. Increase the opacity of the layer to about **80%** and flatten the image.

Add a Highlight

Let's add a highlight to enhance the cylindrical shape.

6. Make a vertical selection of the center third of the can, extending from the lower edge of the top rim to the bottom of the can. Figure 10.4 shows the selection marquee and the highlight effect you are about to create. Choose the Gradient tool with the Foreground to Transparent preset and the Reflected style. Use white as your foreground color. Drag from the center of the selection horizontally to either edge of the selection.

TIP

The Foreground to Transparent preset is a great choice for making a fill that fades into the original image. All gradients are created with a click-and-drag maneuver. Your click establishes the pixel where the first or foreground color begins. The last, or background, color (in this case, full transparency) is set where you release at the end of the drag.

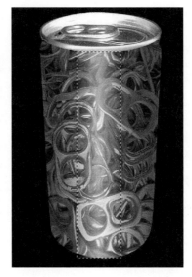

Figure 10.4
Taking a shine to a soft drink.

Create the Logo

Time to add the logo. You can find an authentic one on the unofficial website for Tab groupies: http://home.epix.net/~tjwagner/tab.html. Then add the letter "s" to spell "Tabs." I'll create a similar logo from scratch.

TaBs

Figure 10.5
The beginning of the logo.

7. Use File, New (Cmd/Ctrl+N) to make a white RGB file about 5 inches wide by 2.5 inches high at 72ppi.

8. Choose the Type tool and type **TaBs** in the Blue Highway typeface. Enter **200** for point size and choose Bold style in the Options bar. Reduce the size of the "B" and "s" slightly by dragging over them with the Type tool and typing **170** in the point size field. Figure 10.5 shows the text in black. We can change its color later.

9. Use Layer, Simplify Layer to rasterize the type. Now it's a standard layer, just pixels.

Figure 10.6
The logo is developing…

Figure 10.7
The letters are flat. Hope the soda pop is still fizzy.

10. Let's tighten up that letter spacing, something we couldn't do while the letters were still text. (Photoshop CS users do have that capability, called *tracking*.) Make a rectangular selection around the "a," and then switch to the Move tool. Use the left arrow key to nudge it closer to the "T." Do the same for "B" and "s."

11. We need to extend the right side of the crossbar on the "T" so that it reaches completely across the width of the "a." Make a rectangular selection of the entire crossbar and switch to the Move tool. Hold down both the Shift key and the Option/Alt key, then drag to the right. You are dragging a copy of the selection. Figure 10.6 shows our logo developing.

Modify the Letters

We're going to make parts of the letters "a" and "s" flat instead of curved. Zoom in to **200%** for the next few steps and refer to Figure 10.7 for guidance. If your logo isn't perfect, don't worry. When it's mounted on the can, imperfections won't show.

12. Make a rectangular selection on the upper curve of the "a" and paint the white area with black.

13. Select, Inverse and use the Eraser (or paint with white) to eliminate the bottom edge of the curve.

More Modifications

Do a similar maneuver to reshape the bottom of the "a." By now, altering the "s" should be easy.

14. To make a gap where the remaining curve meets the vertical part of the letter "a," use a thin vertical selection and delete. Do the same to create a gap on the letter "B."

15. Drag and drop your finished logo to the can image.

Wrap the Logo

We need to create a curve for the logo to match the curve of the can. The Warp Text feature is no longer available because the logo hasn't been editable text since step 9. I've got a cool solution.

16. Make the background (can layer) active and use Image, Rotate, 90 degrees Left to turn the can on its side. Then rotate the logo slightly with the Move tool. Figure 10.8 shows the reclining can.

17. Choose Filter, Distort, Shear. Drag the center anchor point on the grid as shown in Figure 10.9. It might take a couple of tries to get the right amount of curvature. For more control, add anchor points to the curve in the grid by clicking on it.

Figure 10.8
The can in its new position.

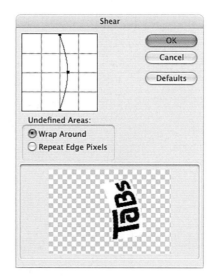

Figure 10.9
Our logo, now in the round.

Figure 10.10
The can flipped back to its original position, with a facelift (reminds me of politics).

18. Rotate the can back to the upright position. Use the Magic Wand to select the white portion of the logo and delete it. Select, Inverse and fill the lettering with your choice of color. Figure 10.10 shows my logo in cola color.

You can fatten letters up or slim them down using one of the Modify commands in the Select menu. With the letters selected, use Select, Modify, Expand and specify the number of pixels. Use Edit, Fill with the same color to create full-figured letters, or a different color to make a border. For thinner letters use Select, Modify, Contract. Inverse the selection and delete.

B B

S S

More B and less S.

19. A few finishing touches will result in an image similar to Figure 10.11. Trim away the excess lettering hanging over the edge of the can by selecting with the Polygon Lasso tool and deleting it. Add a highlight to the logo with the technique from step 6. Finally, replace the solid background with a gradient. Select the background with the Magic Wand and choose a foreground color. The Foreground to Transparent gradient preset is already active and works nicely when you switch to the Linear style and drag from the top to the bottom of the image.

Figure 10.11
See what you can accomplish with a canny approach and some recycled images?

Now you've got a great graphic for a poster or T-shirt. If you want to mount it on a can, use the layout in this image for guidance. Add a Nutrition Facts box and product code for an authentic flavor.

That's a wrap.

Project 2: **Bugs for Breakfast?**

Let's make the box for a cereal called "Yucky Swarms," with insects instead of the usual marshmallow bits. If you've already done the baked potato bug project in the Kid Stuff chapter you'll have a leg up, possibly six legs up.

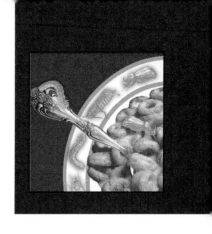

Figure 10.12
Breakfast of scorpions.

Examine the finished piece in Figure 10.12. We'll imitate the Lucky Charms box in several ways: layout, colors, logo, lettering, and product shot.

1. Make a new blank RGB file 7" wide and 10" high at 72ppi. You can work at higher resolution if you prefer to make a better quality print to mount on an actual cereal box.

2. Fill the entire image with a bright saturated red. I'm using a color with these RGB values: **R175 G0 B31**.

3. Use the Polygon Lasso tool to select the inverted triangle shape at the top of the box. Fill it with a pale blue green: **R208 G235 B205**.

4. Use the Elliptical Marquee tool to make the large curved shape, which will become the bowl. For better control, hold the Option/Alt key down to drag from the center and the Shift key to constrain your selection to a perfect circle. You can move the selection into position as long as you have any selection tool active.

Fun with Shapes and Color

Figure 10.13 shows the basic shapes and colors laid out.

Figure 10.14 shows three different typographic looks used on earlier versions of the package. I did some cutting and pasting to explore alternative names. They are useful references as we search for a compatible font.

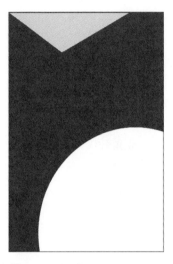

Figure 10.13
We could stop now and hang it in a modern art gallery.

> **TIP**
>
> Let's focus on the "Lucky harms" sample, on the upper right. It will be the easiest to imitate. It is a *sans serif* typeface, literally without those little feet or decorative endings on a stroke. The letterforms are of a uniform bold thickness and perfectly vertical rather than *italic* (slanted). They are *condensed* (tall and narrow). They have a large *x-height*, the height of a lowercase letter relative to its *ascenders* (such as the top of the "h") or *descenders* (like the bottom of the "y"). The *tracking* (letter spacing) and *leading* (line spacing) are both very tight.
>
> Chances are you have a typeface called Tahoma in the basic font set on your computer. It's reasonably similar to the sample, although the shape of the "y" is way off. Find a better match if you can. Fortunately, there are so many other elements on the box, it isn't critical to imitate the font exactly.

Figure 10.14
You could also build "Smarmy Chunks."

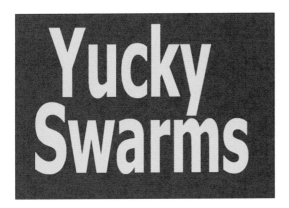

Figure 10.15
Before kerning.

5. Change the foreground color to bright golden yellow: **R247 G204 B38**. Choose the Type tool and type **Yucky Swarms** in 48pt Tahoma Bold. Reduce the leading so the two lines are close together and place them in position on the layout. Leading controls are found between the alignment options and the color menu. Center alignment is fine. You can use the Move tool to change the proportions of the text block. The text is shown in Figure 10.15.

Faux Kerning

There's a little too much space between the "Y" and the "u." The Type tool in Photoshop Elements does not offer *kerning*, adjusting space between letter pairs. We'll do "faux kerning" by hand.

6. Layer, Simplify Layer will turn the text into pixels. Use the Magic Wand with Contiguous on and click on the letter "Y." Switch to the Move tool and use the right arrow to nudge it until the spacing looks right. Flatten the image.

Fix the Bowl

Let's work on the bowl. First, we'll make the two bands decorating the rim.

7. Use this blue green for your foreground color: **R76 G169 B202**.

8. Select the white shape with the Magic Wand. Edit, Stroke Selection using a width of about 16 pixels and Location set to Outside.

9. Select the blue band with the Magic Wand. Copy and paste it. Position and resize it as shown in Figure 10.16. Flatten the image.

10. Open the **cereal.jpg** and **spoon.jpg** images shown in Figure 10.17. Erase or delete everything on the cereal image but the actual Cheerios and a little milk.

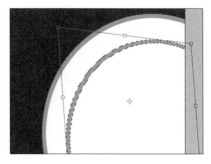

Figure 10.16
I'm with the band.

The Magic Eraser is ideal for eliminating unwanted pixels in this image quickly. It shares a space with the standard Eraser tool and acts just like the Magic Wand, but doesn't merely select pixels. It sends them to oblivion, leaving transparency behind. The first image is the result of just a few clicks. All that's needed is a little cleaning up along the edges with the standard eraser, as in the second image.

Figure 10.17
Should we be concerned about bran recognition?
(Photos courtesy of ShutterStock.)

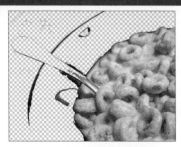

Clean up your plate.

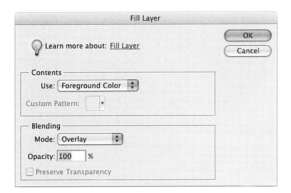

Figure 10.18
Try the Vivid Light blending mode for extreme crunch!

Figure 10.19
Toasty and tasty.

Figure 10.20
Hand me a spoon.

Change the Foreground Color

Cheerios don't look enough like Lucky Charms cereal, so we'll make them darker and more crunchy looking.

11. Change your foreground color to this cocoa brown shade: **R122 G50 B50**. Edit, Fill Layer using the settings shown in Figure 10.18. Notice the blending mode is Overlay. Figure 10.19 shows the result.

12. Drag and drop the cereal image to your composite with the Move tool and position it on the box, as shown in Figure 10.20.

13. Clean up the spoon image by removing the shadow and white background. A combination of erasing and select/delete maneuvers should do it. You'll probably have to do some more cleanup after you see it against the red cereal box in the next step.

14. Drag and drop it to the composite with the Move tool. Rotate the spoon to the angle shown in Figure 10.21 by dragging a corner handle of the bounding box when the cursor looks like a curved double-headed arrow. Reduce the opacity of the spoon layer temporarily so you can see where to erase some Cheerios shapes. This will create the illusion that cereal is in the spoon.

Make a Logo

To make the company logo at the top of the box, you could photograph or scan a real logo graphic and drop it into your composite. I'll create something similar with a script font. Scripts look more or less like cursive handwriting.

15. Choose the Type tool and type **Generic Mealworm** in French Script or Linoscript. Leave enough space between the two words for a large capital "G." The big "G" needs to be made on another text layer. Figure 10.22 shows the logo in the same color you used for the rim of the bowl.

Color Your Bugs

The traditional colors for marshmallow bits (yellow, pink, green, and orange) will be applied to the insects in Figure 10.23.

16. Open the insect images in the **cereal bug** folder available for download from the book's website. They are similar to the ones I'm using. Sorry, but the original bugs crawled away.

Figure 10.21
Got milk? (you had to know that was coming.)

Figure 10.22
Finally ready for the marshmallow bugs.

Figure 10.23
Psst! Fellas, isn't that a talent scout?

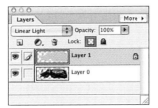

Figure 10.24
Pretty in pink.

Figure 10.25
Why do the other stag beetles keep teasing me?

Figure 10.26
My pupa can beat up your pupa!

17. Let's start with the beetle. Use the Magic Eraser to eliminate most of the background with a few clicks. Switch to the standard Eraser tool to remove the remaining background pixels.

18. Make a new layer and change foreground color to the pink used for marshmallow hearts: **R251 G171 B182**. Edit, Fill Layer in Normal mode at **100%**. Change the blending mode of the layer to Linear Light.

19. Here's how to remove the pink background from the layer. Use the Magic Wand to select the white background on the beetle. Target the color layer and delete. Figure 10.24 shows your Layers palette at this point.

20. Your finished beetle is shown in Figure 10.25. Flatten the file. Click on the white background with the Magic Wand and Select, Inverse to select the bug. Drag it to the cereal box with the Move tool. Resize, rotate, and position it on the rim of the bowl.

21. Repeat steps 17 through 20 for the caterpillar, using the orange associated with stars: **R255 G118 B9**. See Figure 10.26 for the tasty result.

Use green for the grasshopper. Some of the original colors still show after the Linear Light layer is in place. Copy the color layer and switch to Hard Light mode. The image shows your Layers palette after that maneuver.

How green can you go?

Yellow Fly Fever

Yellow is the only color left, so we'll use that on the housefly. The yellow from your text will work fine. It took considerable experimenting before I got the fly color just right. Here's the recipe.

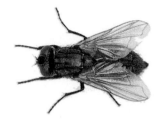

Figure 10.27
Be afraid. Be very afraid.

22. Use Edit, Fill Layer with the foreground color (yellow) in Color mode at **100%**. Figure 10.27 shows this stage.

23. Add two color layers, as you did for the grasshopper. This time, use Hard Light mode at **35%** opacity for one layer and Overlay mode at about **80%** opacity for the other. See Figure 10.28 for my solution to the fly problem.

Figure 10.28
"Help me!"

Create Bug Shadows

Let's put a drop shadow under each bug, so they won't look painted on but ready to crawl around at any moment. You'll only need to do one, then you can copy and paste the effect on the other bugs.

24. Target any one of the insect layers on the rim of the bowl. Choose the Layer Styles category from the Styles and Effects palette, then open the Drop Shadows library. Apply the Low style. Your layers palette will now have a little "f" icon indicating that there is an effect on that layer. Double-click the "f" icon to get the Style Settings dialog and reduce Shadow Distance to zero pixels, as shown in Figure 10.29.

Figure 10.29
"Style me!"

Figure 10.30
The caterpillar might be facing the wrong way.

25. Use the Layer, Layer Style, Copy Layer Style command and then the Paste Layer Style command on each of the other bug layers. Figure 10.30 has the rim of the bowl complete. Whew!

The Final Touch

We can easily sprinkle a few bugs on the cereal in the bowl.

26. Use the Move tool and hold down the Option/Alt key while you drag a copy of each bug to a new location. Use Rotate commands to flip the layers in various directions.

Serve Your Yucky Swarms

See Figure 10.31 for the finished product. Notice that I had a fly land on the company logo and a caterpillar crawl up the spoon (or maybe it's going down).

> **NOTE**
> Print the final image on letter-size self-adhesive paper. Then mount it on a real cereal box and watch for reactions from the whole family. Bon Apetit!

Figure 10.31
Part of a healthy breakfast…for frogs.

Project 1:
**Olde Tyme
Photography**

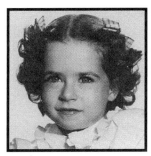

Project 2:
Pre-War Portraits

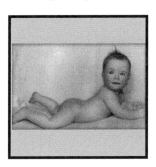

Project 3:
Naked Babies

Chapter 11

Artsy-Craftsy

Turn real-life scrapbooking into its digital equivalent. Your hands will stay clean, you won't risk exposure to toxic chemicals, and you'll never run out of photo corners. Digitize, organize, and colorize those old family portraits tucked away in a shoebox. Better yet, work with fresh digital photos and make them look as if they've been lying around in a shoebox for decades.

Project 1: **Olde Tyme Photography**

Figure 11.1 is a photo of my grandmother circa 1914. Figure 11.2 is a photo of me circa 1975 at a resort concession. I got into a period costume, posed, and came back in about an hour for the sepia toned print in a cardboard frame. Pretty good imitation of turn of the century (the previous century) style and technology.

Let's take a much more recent color photo and age it. I'll be working with the image of my niece in Figure 11.3, and you can use somebody in your family.

Figure 11.1
Ninety years ago.

Figure 11.2
Seems like yesterday.

Figure 11.3   **Nesa, about 10 years before the prom picture in Chapter 3.**

Figure 11.4
Looking older already.

1. Open the Photographic Effects library in the Layer Styles category on the Styles and Effects palette. Click on Sepia Tone, and you'll be prompted to turn the image into a layer. Click OK, and click OK again to dismiss the dialog box asking you to name the layer.

Add Authenticity

Not surprisingly, all the color is replaced by sepia, as seen in Figure 11.4.

> **TIP**
>
> Photoshop CS users, as well as you Elements people, can make a sepia tone by using a dark brown foreground color and the Edit, Fill Layer (or Fill Selection) command. Choose Color for the blending mode and 100% opacity in the Fill dialog box. This method gives you much more control, as there are only nine tones to choose from in Photographic Effects but the Fill command gives you access to millions of colors.

An authentic old photo is likely to have cracks or streaks or some kind of damage. We can fake that.

2. Make a copy of the layer by dragging it to the New Layer icon on the Layers palette.

3. Use Filter, Texture, Craquelure with settings similar to those in Figure 11.5.

4. Erase any unwanted cracks or artifacts on the face, revealing the unblemished sepia layer.

Create a Vignette

An oval vignette (pronounced "vin yet") will help suggest the period we're imitating.

5. Drag a vertical ellipse selection around the head and shoulders. Double-click on Vignette in the Frames library of Effects for the result shown in Figure 11.6. If you want an even softer edge, use Select, Feather and set the number of pixels for the blended edge before you apply the Vignette command. Incidentally, I painted out that annoying railing behind Nesa with the Clone Stamp tool.

> **TIP**
>
> Photoshop CS users can easily make a vignette from scratch. After feathering the oval selection Select, Inverse. Press Delete/Backspace to fill with the background color.

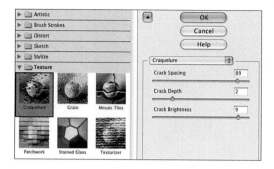

Figure 11.5
Just a few patches of damage, please.

Figure 11.6
Is this oval kid thinking about becoming an oval teen?

Figure 11.7
That white layer gives me an idea.

Figure 11.8
Mmm... creamy!

Figure 11.9
A blank expression.

Fill in the Layer

The automatic Vignette frame creates the layers shown in Figure 11.7. Let's fill that stark white layer with something warmer and older.

6. Use the Eyedropper tool to sample a light tone from the face. Target the white layer and fill with the Paint Bucket. Now the background is a lovely antique cream shade, shown in Figure 11.8.

Create a Frame

Let's make a frame.

7. Target the top layer and click on the transparent area with the Magic Wand. Select, Inverse and you have the oval selected.

8. Return to the Frames library. Double-click on Cut Out. Several operations will be done automatically, and the result is shown in Figure 11.9.

I'm not sure what I expected; certainly not this. But let's not rush to Undo just yet. Glance at the Layers palette, shown here. Nesa's face is still there, on the background. What would make it show through the opaque white oval on the layer above? If you've already worked some of the other chapters, take a moment to think about blending modes.

We have to make that white oval transparent, but how?

9. Switch from the default Normal blending mode for the layer to Darken. The face is darker than the white oval, so it wins. The new border is darker than the creamy background, so it wins, too. How cool was that? See Figure 11.10.

Figure 11.10
A win-win situation. In the accent of my grandmother, a "vin, yet."

Project 2: **Pre-War Portraits**

Prior to the early 1940s when color film became available, colorizing was done by hand with transparent dyes. Figure 11.11 is a good example. We can imitate this look with Photoshop.

Figure 11.11
Me in 1942, cute as a button.

1. If you don't have a vintage portrait of your own to colorize, open **Rhoda1944.jpg**, available for download from the *Fun with Photoshop Elements 3* website, shown in Figure 11.12.

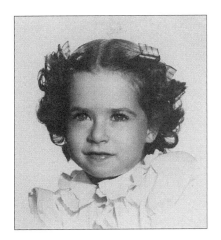

Figure 11.12
Me again, still cute.

2. Make a small blank RGB file for a palette of colors to test and for convenience while you're working. Fill small rectangles with a few possible skin tones and colors for eyes, hair, and clothing. My palette is shown in Figure 11.13.

3. Use the Brush tool with Color for the blending mode. Set the brush size large enough to cover a lot of ground smoothly but still have control over details. I'm using a Soft Round brush about the size of the nose. Choose a skin tone and make a test stroke on the face, at about **50%** opacity. Undo if necessary and change opacity or color until you like the result.

Use Opacity to Modify Coloration

Figure 11.14 on the left has the test I made with the first three colors on my palette at **100%** opacity. I liked the middle orangey one, but reduced it to **45%**.

4. When you have the color and opacity you like, paint the entire face in a single stroke, eyes and all, to avoid streakiness from overlapping strokes. Zoom in to **200%** for more control and to spot any problems.

Figure 11.13
Your colors may vary.

> **TIP**
>
> Make brush size changes quickly using the right and left bracket keys: []. To switch colors without leaving the Brush tool, hold down the Option/Alt key and click on the desired sample in your color palette, or anywhere. The only other tool you might need for this project is the Sponge, to desaturate (reduce the strength of a color) in some areas. You'll find the Sponge at the bottom of the Tools palette, hanging out with his darkroom buddies, Dodge and Burn.

 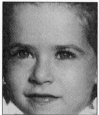 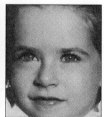

Figure 11.14
Testing and tinting.

Figure 11.15
Young, gifted, and very blue-eyed.

5. Build up color where needed, like cheeks and lips. Figure 11.14 center shows lips working nicely after another layer of the same color and same opacity, with a smaller brush. But the cheek color has harsh edges that need to be repaired with the Sponge. Work those edges carefully with the Sponge at low opacity. Too much desaturation will give your skin an unhealthy gray look. The right side of Figure 11.14 shows the cheek color smoothed out and the eyes painted blue-green, accurately I might add.

6. You can probably paint the hair at **100%** opacity. Watch for transition areas between skin and hair.

7. I painted the blouse yellow at **50%** and used **75%** for the hair ribbons.

8. A very gradual vignette edge is typical of this period. Layering low opacity strokes to build up color can accomplish fading color at the edges. Start at the outer edge and begin each layer closer to the beginning of the fade. See Figure 11.15 for the finished piece.

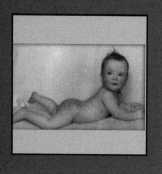

Project 3: **Naked Babies**

If you ever had a baby, or just been a baby, you must have some pictures similar to the one in Figure 11.16. I'll rely on you to find your own source image for this project. That's so I can't be accused of posting kiddy porn on the Internet.

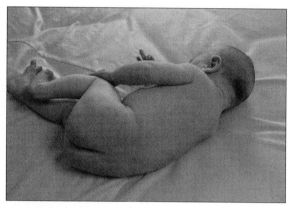

Figure 11.16
Miranda in the raw. (Photo courtesy of Barbara Pollack.)

I. Click on the Create Adjustment Layer icon in the Layers palette and choose Levels.

This is a good place to start adjusting the range of values (brightness). You'll see a histogram like the one in this image indicating the distribution of image pixels from black to white. Sure enough, the whitest point in the image falls short of the maximum. Move the white triangle to the left until it meets the right edge of the histogram. It wouldn't hurt to pull the black triangle slightly to the right to extend the dark end of the range.

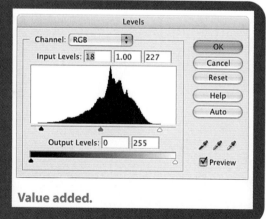

Value added.

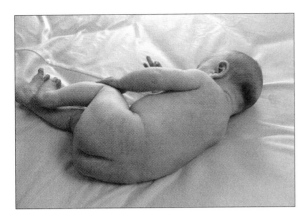

Figure 11.17
If I could walk at all, I wouldn't need talcum powder.

TIP

Here's how it works. The white rectangle to the right of the adjustment layer icon is the layer mask. White means "on" and black means "off." So, painting with black on the layer mask turns the adjustment off for those pixels. Yes, you can paint them back "on" with white.

2. Create an Adjustment layer for Brightness/Contrast. I set the Brightness to **+19** and the Contrast to **+9**. These settings can be changed at any time by double-clicking the adjustment layer to get the sliders again. You could also reduce the amount with the Opacity control on the Layers palette.

Remove Redness

The brighter highlights on the sheets and the pinker glow to the baby in Figure 11.17 look good. Unfortunately, the diaper rash got enhanced, too! Photoshop Elements has a tool for fixing red eye, but not red tush. No, the Healing Brush won't work, but I have a solution.

3. Target the Levels adjustment layer and choose the Brush tool in Normal mode with your choice of opacity. With black as the foreground color, paint over any areas where you want to reduce or eliminate the levels change.

The first figure shows the Layers palette after I cured the diaper rash. Notice the black area on the layer mask. The second figure has a close-up after the soothing treatment. If we could see her face, she'd be smiling.

Black is the new pink.

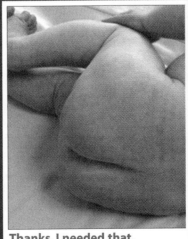

Thanks, I needed that.

Mat Finish

Now let's make the frame shown in Figure 11.18, using another naked baby.

4. Use Image, Resize, Canvas Size to add more space around the entire image.

5. Create a new layer and fill it with pink or another color you prefer for the inner mat. Reduce opacity temporarily so you can see the baby. Make a rectangular selection slightly inside the edges of the baby. Delete it, and you have cut the hole in the mat. Return to **100%** opacity but don't flatten the image.

6. Open the Drop Shadows library of Layer Styles and apply a Low drop shadow to the mat. The effect is too strong, so let's adjust it. Double-click on the little "f" (for "effects") icon on the Layers palette to get the Style Settings controls. Reduce Shadow Distance to 2 or 3 pixels. Figure 11.19 shows the mat with an adjusted shadow.

7. To make the outer mat, open the Textures library in the Effects category and double-click on Gold Sprinkles. A new layer will be created automatically with this spectacular surface. Once again, reduce opacity so you can see the baby and make a rectangular selection big enough to allow an edge of the pink mat to show. Delete the selection for the double mat effect.

8. Repeat step 6 for the drop shadow, or copy the adjusted shadow from the pink mat and paste it to the gold one. Those commands are in the Layer, Layer Style menu at the top of your screen.

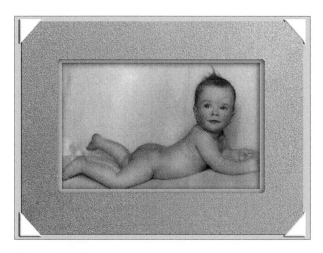

Figure 11.18
Guess who!

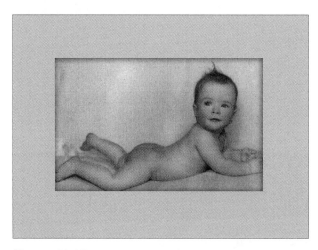

Figure 11.19
I don't wear that much lipstick anymore.

9. Double-click Photo Corners in the Frames library of Effects and sit back to watch them constructed automatically (all four of them at once!).

10. There is a generic medium gray behind the photo corners, which can (and should) be changed. Select it with the Magic Wand and fill with any other color (quickly, please, that gray is awful).

Project 1:
Come Up and See My Filters

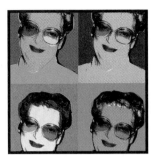

Project 2:
Mom and Pop Art

Project 3:
Make a Good Impressionist

Chapter 12

Artsy-Phartsy

Turn any photo into a work of art. Imitate traditional, modern, and postmodern styles. Do you dream of becoming the next Rembrandt or Picasso? (I'm not talking about Joe Rembrandt or Betty Picasso.) Don't bother to stretch canvasses, pour turpentine, or rent a loft. Just sit down and create.

Project 1: **Come Up and See My Filters**

If you like instant gratification but are trying to cut down on carbs, play with Photoshop's Filter Gallery for an hour or two. First, we'll apply a classic drawing medium to a basic figure study.

1. Open **beachguy.jpg**, shown in Figure 12.1, or work with the nude model you prefer.

2. Use the Eyedropper tool to sample a reddish brown from the midtone range of his skin to serve as the foreground color. Or enter these values in the Color Picker: **R103 G49 B3**. The background color should be white.

Figure 12.1
A traditional subject for drawing, and low in carbs. (Photo courtesy of ShutterStock.)

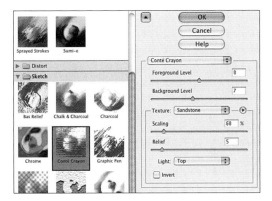

Figure 12.2
The apple icons show each effect, even if you're not using a Mac.

3. Filter, Filter Gallery will give you access to a wide variety of styles, organized by category. Open the Sketch category and click on Conté Crayon. Zoom out by clicking the minus sign in the lower-left corner of the preview box. Use the settings shown in Figure 12.2. The result is shown in Figure 12.3.

TIP

The green apple thumbnail image is a visual cue for each effect. (Photoshop CS users will see a multicolor windsurfing sail instead of the green apple.) Most filters retain the original colors, so the apple stays green. The Sketch category is special. With only a couple of exceptions, the apples are blue and white, where blue represents your current foreground color and white stands in for the background color. Conté Crayon, along with the Chalk & Charcoal filter, also provides a gray midtone.

Figure 12.3
A classic drawing in a click.

Conté crayons are compressed pigment sticks, typically brown or reddish brown, that are firmer than chalks or pastels. The traditional technique uses medium gray or tinted paper with a textured surface. Forms are developed with dark strokes and highlights are added with white. This image shows the excellent still life drawing you can get with this filter.

Print this to get an "A" in a basic drawing class. (Photo courtesy of ArtExplosion.)

Simplify Me

Let's use another filter to turn the musician in Figure 12.4 into an abstract work of art.

4. Open **clarinetplayer.jpg**, and find Cutout in the Artistic category of the Filter Gallery.

NOTE

Notice that there are three settings for the Cutout effect. When you reduce Number of Levels, lower Edge Fidelity and increase Edge Simplicity, you can get abstract in a hurry.

Figure 12.4
My brother Mark can play the Macedonian bagpipe, too. (Photo courtesy of Mark Levy.)

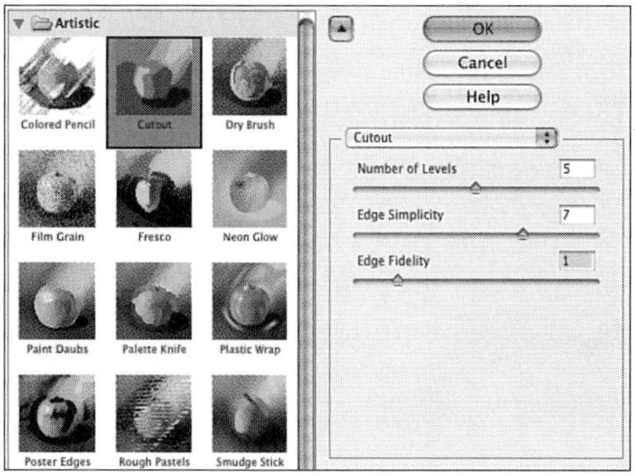

Figure 12.5
Sliders set to 5, 7, and 1. You should also try 3, 6, 1 and 4, 7, 2.

5. Move the sliders around in various combinations to explore the possibilities. Use the settings shown in Figure 12.5 to get the image in Figure 12.6.

Figure 12.6
Still a musician, barely, but not my brother anymore.

Project 2: **Mom and Pop Art**

You don't have to be a superstar or glamorpuss like Liz and Marilyn to get the Andy Warhol treatment. You can be a little old Jewish lady in Florida. No, it's not me this time. I live in California. We'll create a bold graphic version of my mom from the **Ida.jpg** file. Better still, use a close-up headshot of your own mom.

I. Change the color photo into grayscale. Like most actions in Photoshop, there's more than one way to do this. It's easiest to simply use Enhance, Adjust Color, Remove Color and click OK. Photoshop CS users will find Image, Adjustments, Desaturate does the trick. Figure 12.7 shows the photo before and after color removal.

Figure 12.7
Gray-haired and grayscale. (Photo courtesy of Ida Levy.)

This image previews the finished effect. The Warhol silkscreen look has a few flat color fills with hard edges and just enough of the original photo to maintain a likeness.

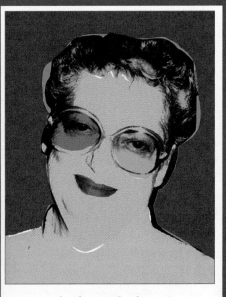

I'm a work of art! Who knew?

Figure 12.8
Starting to feel a little flat.

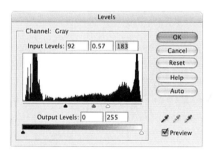

Figure 12.9
Suffering from value range compression? This could be why.

Figure 12.10
Level with me.

Flatten the Look

We'll reduce detail and create extremely high contrast in the next step. Use Figure 12.8 as a guide for how much change is needed to get this simplified, flat look.

2. Click on the Create Adjustment Layer icon in the Layers palette and choose Levels. Move both the black and white sliders under the histogram toward the center and adjust the middle gray slider as needed.

   Figure 12.9 shows the adjustments I made to compress the value range and eliminate subtle midtones as much as possible.

3. You still have control over the Levels adjustment. Double-click the adjustment layer to fiddle with sliders again, or simply change opacity in the Layers palette, shown in Figure 12.10.

Get Edgy

Look at the high contrast stage again, and notice that the hair blends into the black background. We need to make the background much lighter in contrast with the hair. We will begin to develop the hard-edge look at the same time.

TIP

The standard Lasso tool can also function like the Polygon Lasso when you hold down the Option/Alt key. You'll be able to drag for a freehand line and do point-to-point clicks for straight line portions of the selection. This technique is ideal for the next step.

4. Target the background layer. Use the Lasso tool while pressing the Option/Alt key to select the black area behind Ida, making a bold irregular shape around the head and face. Your selection should look imperfect, like it might have been cut out with scissors that were too big for detailed work.

5. Fill the selection with medium or light gray, using either the Paint Bucket tool or the Edit, Fill command. Your work should look something like Figure 12.11 at this stage.

6. Commit to the Levels adjustment with the Flatten Image command in the Layers palette menu. While you're there, make a new layer. Set the blending mode to Darken or Multiply. You can experiment with other blending modes later.

7. Open the Default set of Color Swatches, available in the Window menu and shown in Figure 12.12. This will be handy for changing color without having to open the Color Picker.

8. Use the Lasso tool to make the same kind of bold, imperfect selection you made in step 3, this time for the hair.

9. Choose the Paint Bucket tool and click on a bright saturated color in the Color Swatches. I chose green. Fill the selection by clicking inside the selected area on the layer. Another way to fill a selection with the foreground color is with keystrokes: Option/Alt+Delete/Backspace.

Figure 12.11
You call this a haircut?

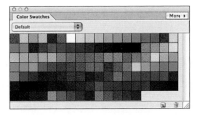

Figure 12.12
Swatches? We don't need no stinkin' swatches!

Figure 12.13
Differently colored lenses in the eyeglasses might not be a Warhol thing. It's my thing.

10. Repeat steps 8 and 9 for each major shape. Figure 12.13 shows my color layer with visibility of the background turned off. (The little eyeball icon in the Layers palette toggles visibility.) All shapes are filled with color except the face. No need to make a selection at this point. Just click with the Paint Bucket to fill the remaining shape with a new color.

NOTE

Peek at the image in the previous sidebar again. I used Darken mode for the color layer. This would be a good time to explore other blending modes in addition to Darken and Multiply. Linear Dodge and Hard Light are promising possibilities. Try Difference mode for something really wacky.

A grid of variations on the same image is very much in the Warhol tradition, as in this image. It's quick and easy to make alternate color combinations once you have the fills completed. Use Color Swatches and the Paint Bucket to fill the shapes you already have. Blending mode variations will work nicely, too.

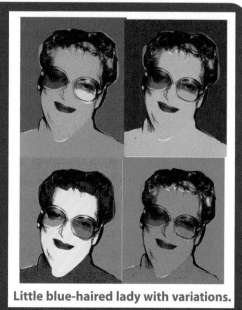

Little blue-haired lady with variations.

Project 3: **Make a Good Impressionist**

There are a few filters in the Artistic category that imitate painterly effects, but they must be applied globally to the entire image or selection. If you want to apply a painting style the old-fashioned way (one brushstroke at a time) you'll need the Impressionist Brush. It shares a space with the Brush tool.

If you're a Sunday painter, here are some landscape studies you can do any day of the week, rain or shine. We'll start with the low-key photo of a sailboat near a pier, shown in Figure 12.14.

1. Open **nightpier.jpg**. Make a copy of the image on another layer by dragging the background to the New Layer icon. You'll paint on the layer, and the original will stay unchanged in case you want to redo parts of the image.

2. Choose the Impressionist Brush. To get results similar to Figure 12.15, load the Natural Brushes 2 presets and pick Chalk-Light. I used the default size, 50px. Paint the upper half of the image with the Loose Medium style and the lower half with Tight Medium.

Figure 12.14
Dock of the bay. (Photo courtesy of ShutterStock.)

Figure 12.15
Muddy waters.

The Impressionist Brush moves existing colors around based on your choice of style under More Options, the brush preset you use, and, of course, the movement of your stylus. The first image is a sampler showing just a few possibilities.

Each rectangle began with a Tie Dye pattern fill (upper left). Here's a key to the Brush presets and Impressionist stroke styles used. Preset libraries other than the default are in parentheses.

- Top row: All three samples use the Hard Round 13px preset. From left to right the styles are Dab, Loose Medium, and Loose Curl.

- Middle row: Chalk 23px with Dab style, Dune Grass with any style, Rough Ink (Wet Media Brushes) with Tight Short style.

- Bottom row: Stipple 21px (Natural Brushes) with Loose Long style, Pastel Light (Natural Brushes 2) with Loose Long style, Wet Brush 20px (Natural Brushes 2) with Loose Curl style.

The second image shows a portion of the Options bar for the Impressionist brush. I recommend matching the Area setting to your brush size. Default Tolerance is fine.

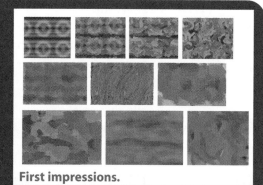

First impressions.

And... there's more!

Resurrect Original Details with the Clone Brush

The brushstrokes have made the sky and water look interesting but the boat has gotten too blurred and amorphous. I'm glad I have that pristine version underneath.

3. Choose the Clone Stamp tool with Aligned checked in the Options bar. Click on the original background image to make it the active layer. Hold down the Option/Alt key and click on a pixel that corresponds to something still visible in the painted version. This establishes the source you'll be cloning with.

4. Click on the painted layer in the Layers palette to make it active, and start cloning strokes at about the same point. You'll know it by the crosshairs showing the source pixel. Figure 12.16 shows a detail of the painting where some of the original boat has been cloned back for another try.

5. Return to the Impressionist Brush and reduce its size to about **20** pixels. Switch to the Tight Short style. These changes should give you more control when you repaint the boat. My second attempt is shown in Figure 12.17.

Figure 12.16
Ghost ship returns.

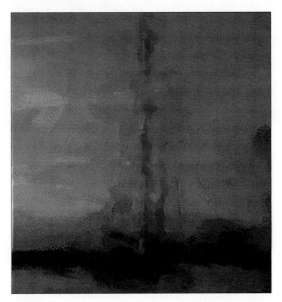

Figure 12.17
If your first impression isn't very impressive....

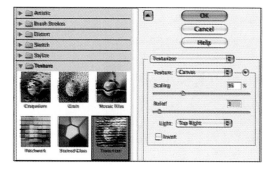

Figure 12.18
Use Sandstone instead of Canvas for the look of watercolor.

6. For a finishing touch, use Filter, Texture, Texturizer to create a canvas surface. Figure 12.18 shows my settings and Figure 12.19 is the oil painting completed.

   Better yet, print the finished image on real canvas. And don't forget to clean your brushes before the paint dries.

Imitate One of the Masters

And now, for my last trick of the evening, here's a way to imitate the style of Georges Seurat. This time we have several boats at the dock or wharf or (I hope) quay, and it's bright daylight.

Figure 12.19
Virtual oil meets ersatz canvas.

Georges would have liked painting this scene. That black dog looks a lot like the one from his most famous work, *Sunday Afternoon on the Island of La Grande Jatte*.

Seurat's *pointillist* technique uses lots of dots in contrasting colors that blend optically at a distance. Photoshop's Impressionist Brush can work only with colors that are already in the image. Until Adobe invents a Neo-Impressionist brush, we'll have to add colorful dots first.

Sunday afternoon with a French dog? (Photo courtesy of ArtExplosion.)

7. Open **boats.jpg**, similar to the image I'm using, or another colorful photo you prefer. Apply Filter, Noise, Add Noise using about **50%** for amount and a Gaussian distribution. Do *not* check Monochromatic. Figure 12.20 has the colorful dotty version.

8. Choose the Impressionist Brush with Dab or Tight Short for Style and the Hard Round 5 or 9 pixels preset. Paint over the entire image. Scribbling is fine; no need to be careful. Be sure you don't miss a spot. The fake *pointillism* effect in Figure 12.21 is (um) spot on.

Figure 12.20
Pre-Impressionist.

Figure 12.21
Post-Impressionist, or "Quay Seurat!"

Appendix A

Resources

Maybe you finished working through the projects, or you're just browsing through the book before you buy, or you always start reading from the back. Anyhow, this section suggests some sources where you can find images to play with, media to print on, and even places to display your work to other *Photoshoppers*. (Sorry, Adobe, I tried so hard not to use that word!)

Searching the Internet for Images

Need a variety of images, or something specific, in a hurry? If you don't mind low resolution, and are careful about possible copyright issues, use Google's image search. When you get to the Google home page at **www.google.com**, click on Images and type in what you're looking for. This is a great way to get visual references for accuracy, or just browse for ideas. I googled "breakfast cereal" to prepare for the *Lucky Charms* parody in Chapter 10 and saw bowlfuls of flakes and toasted what-nots as well as product shots of boxes, including some political parodies I'd rather not talk about if you don't mind.

There are commercial online sources for high-resolution images. They generally require payment of fees for specified usage and their target market is graphics professionals. If you want a lot of images, those fees can really add up. For high-quality images with a liberal licensing agreement, and at bargain prices, my vote goes to ShutterStock.com. It's easy to use their Boolean search engine to find what you need quickly and, best of all, you can subscribe for a small fee and have *unlimited downloads* for your subscription period. One month of this all-you-can-eat service costs about $120 last time I checked. Take a look: **http://www.shutterstock.com**

Many of the images used in this book are available for download from the *Fun with Photoshop Elements 3* website at **www.samspublishing.com**. Type the book's ISBN (0672327309) in the Search field to find the page you're looking for. Some of the projects invite you to provide your own images. A Google search is an ideal way to acquire images that are similar to those that I use to demonstrate features and techniques.

Using Royalty-Free Stock Images

Many companies offer stock photography or clip art you can purchase in sets based on subject matter. You can do keyword searches online or acquire CDs with images at various resolutions. Be sure you understand the licensing agreement before you buy. Even "copyright-free" sources might include usage limits. Always read the fine print.

A few years ago I spent $100 on an *Art Explosion* collection of more than 500,000 (that's half a million!) pieces of clip art and stock photography that came on 37 disks with a printed catalog 2.5 inches thick! Sure, most of it was garbage, but it has paid for itself over and over again. Here's the website: **www.artexplosion.com**.

Here are the URLs for the other companies that provided some source images for *Fun with Photoshop Elements 3*:

- RubberBall: **www.rubberball.com**
- Corbis: **http://pro.corbis.com**
- BigFoto: **www.bigfoto.com/**

Scanning Images

Take old family photos out of their albums (or the shoebox) and digitize them. Basic scanners were really cheap the last time I checked, and this is a handy device to have around. If you want to scan printed images from books or magazine, your scanner should have a Descreen feature. This is used to prevent a *moiré pattern* from the halftone dots used in process printing.

Printed images are almost certainly copyright protected; not a problem unless you want to publish. When I was just starting to fool around with image manipulation, in the early '90s, I scanned a portrait of a woman that I found in a book of images by a commercial photographer. I came up with a painterly version of the face, and displayed it as a portfolio sample. Not much later a publisher asked to use it as cover art for a technical trade magazine. I wanted the exposure, of course, and convinced myself that I had changed the original enough and nobody would recognize it. Besides, I wouldn't be paid. Shortly after that, I was offered a fee for using the same image in an ad for digitizer tablets. Once again I rationalized that the image was my own. I wasn't sued or anything (if that's what you expected to hear, sorry to disappoint you), but I was taking a risk.

Printing from the Desktop

I've got a cheap Canon i250 inkjet printer that I use for most of my letter-size printing. I can get spectacular results as long as I use high-quality paper and other media. Ordinary paper is too porous, letting ink spread into the fibers so images get blurry or muddy looking.

My choice for crisp rich color is glossy photo paper. Epson and HP make it, among others, and you can order it from stores like Office Depot. It comes in various weights and can be glossy on both sides. Check your printer specs to make sure it can handle a heavy paper.

Office Depot offers a number of self-adhesive "print & stick" paper products for pre-cut labels and bumper stickers, or whole sheets. These are ideal for printing the fake soda can or *Yucky Swarms* cereal box you made in Chapter 10, "Fool Me Twice." Iron-on transfers are also available to print, cut, and peel, then apply to clothing, hats, or what-have-you. And think of the fun you can have making instant refrigerator magnets by printing on magnet sheets.

Archival-quality media are available for fine art printing from your desktop. A great resource is **www.inkjetart.com,** where you can find letter size or larger format canvas (glossy or matte), watercolor paper, and printable fabrics, perfect for inkjet output of your work from Chapter 12, "Artsy-Phartsy." If you know you'll print on canvas, you won't need to add an optical canvas texture to the artwork.

Outsourcing Print Jobs

Sometimes you just need a professional printing job, especially if you want large quantities. I've had business cards and postcards printed from my digital files by a company called 4by6.com. Everything is done online. You choose the format and quantity, download the templates for Photoshop (or a page layout program such as Quark Xpress or InDesign), upload your images and fonts, view the proofs, and you're done.

If you want to print BIG but don't want to invest in a large format printer, order from an outfit like Imagers: **www.imagers.com/poster.html.** Visit their website for a price list of poster sizes from 18×24 to 59×96 printed on photo paper, film, vinyl, or canvas. Another company, youHuge.com, offers poster-size prints that can be mounted on foam core or other boards. Check them out: **http:// youhuge.com/large_format_posters.htm**.

CaféPress is a very cool resource: **www.cafepress.com.** You can arrange to have your Photoshop images printed on clothing, mugs, mouse pads, calendars, and more. Better yet, set up shop and sell your creations to other people! It's free to get started. You just decide the markup over their base price and that's your profit per unit. See the list of products and base prices here: **www.cafepress.com/ cp/info/help/base_prices.aspx**. CafePress.com manufactures your products as they are ordered, ships them, and manages payment.

Fonts

After using the Type tool for a while, you might get a hankering for more exciting typefaces than just the ones installed on your computer at the factory. Lots of fonts are available free for personal use. They can be downloaded quickly from sites like Blue Vinyl fonts: **www.bvfonts.com/free/ freeware.shtml** or Larabie Fonts, where I found the Blue Highway type used for the fake highway signs in Chapter 8, "The Write Stuff": **www.larabiefonts.com**.

Contests

Somebody once said "A picture is worth a thousand words" and somebody else quipped "A picture is worth a thousand words, but it will take longer to download." I'd be happy to tell you who said both of those things if I knew. If you know, tell the folks at Pithy Quotes: **www.stcsig.org/usability/resources/pith.html**. (No, that is not one of the contests.)

I do know who created a website called *Worth 1000.com*, where you can see eye-popping, humorous, and imaginative work by Photoshop users. It's Avi Muchnick. He's the one running the contests. Visit **www.worth1000.com** to participate in intriguing competitions for image manipulators or just browse the images that were submitted. There are contests for beginners, intermediate, advanced, and professional users. Trust me: This website is worth 1,000 visits.

Appendix B

Photoshop in a Peanut Shell

As I mentioned in the introduction, which I'm confident you read carefully, this book doesn't even pretend to cover everything there is to know about Photoshop Elements. The following tips are incomplete as well, but touch on the essential features you'll be using over and over in this book and in real life. This should serve as a quick reference for beginners and a refresher for returning users. These bits of info and insight apply to all incarnations of Photoshop, unless I say different. For in-depth coverage use the online Help feature or (gasp!) the User Manual.

Where Is It?

Tools are arranged in a vertical strip along the left edge of your screen (unless you move it). Similar tools might share a space in the toolbar: For example, the toning tools (Dodge, Burn, and Sponge) are roommates. Options for the currently active tool are arranged in a horizontal strip above your image. Menu commands are found at the top of your screen, and palettes for layers, special effects, and so on are found in the Window menu.

Selection, Selection, Selection

If there is an area on your image that you want to change in some way (size, color, special effects) while protecting other areas from change, you have to select it first. Photoshop is pixel-based, so even though it may walk and quack like a duck, an image of a duck isn't an object: It's just pixels. That's why Photoshop provides several tools for selecting groups of pixels.

I should mention that there is one group of Photoshop tools useful for imitating object-oriented or vector-based graphics. The Rectangle tool (not to be confused with the Rectangular Marquee, a selection tool) shares space with the Line tool and several other vector-like tools such as the Custom Shape tool whose library includes… a duck. When a Photoshop image is flattened, however, everything is just pixels.

Rectangular or Elliptical Marquee

Use to drag a rectangular or oval selection. Hold the Shift key down to constrain the selection to a perfect square or circle.

Lasso Tool

Draw a free-hand selection around an irregular shape. Sharing a space with the Lasso tool is the *Polygon Lasso* for selecting any shape composed of straight-line segments. Just click on each point of the shape. Also available: the *Magnetic Lasso*, handy for selecting a complex shape with a strong edge in contrast to surrounding pixels. Drag the tool's "hot spot" around the edge.

Magic Wand

Use this to make a selection based on color. Works best on areas that are similar in color and contrast strongly with neighboring areas. Just click anywhere and all pixels within the color *Threshold* (adjustable in the Options bar) are selected. You have the option of *Contiguous* (touching) or not.

Managing Selections

Select, Feather to give your selection a soft edge. This is great for creating a vignette or a gradual transition.

Add to a selection by holding down the Shift key while using any selection tool. Subtract from a selection by holding the Option/Alt key down.

Select, Inverse to select what was unselected and vice versa. Figure B.1 shows how useful that can be. The sports car has a complicated outline that you could probably manage with the Magnetic Lasso, but the entire gray background can easily be selected with two or three clicks of the Magic Wand (remember to hold the Shift key down if you need more than one click). At this point, Select, Inverse will select the car.

Figure B.1
Selecting the car is easy. Paying for it is more difficult. (Photo courtesy of ArtExplosion.)

Save your selections in case you need to work with them again, especially if they took a while to make. The *Save Selection* command is in the Select menu, along with the *Load Selection* command for bringing it back, even if the image has been closed.

Layers

Place separate image elements on their own layers so you can manipulate them independently, and you won't need to concern yourself so much with selection. Copy-and-paste or drag-and-drop maneuvers will automatically create a new layer for the item.

Adjustment Layers

You can make layers that alter the look of an image by changing its colors or tonality. These adjustment layers are available in the Layer menu or with the black-and-white circle icon on the Layers palette. They remain adjustable until you commit to them with the *Merge* or *Flatten* commands in the More pop-up menu on the Layers palette.

Blending Modes

By default a layer is 100% opaque and covers what is under it. You can reduce opacity in the Layers palette, where you can also toggle visibility of a layer on or off. More exciting is the pop-up list of blending modes that determine how the pixels of a layer interact with other layers or with the background image. Figure B.2 shows an eagle and Figure B.3 shows a solid red color adjustment layer added.

Figure B.2
America's national bird could have been a turkey.
(Photo courtesy of ArtExplosion.)

Figure B.3
At 100% Normal mode you'd just see red.

Figure B.4 has just a few of the possible variations resulting from a change of blending mode. The upper row is Lighten mode, followed by Darken mode. The lower left shows Overlay and the lower right a dramatic Vivid Light mode.

Figure B.4
Eeny, meeny, miney, mode.

Brushes

The Brush tool has a wide array of options, including all the blending modes available to layers. Brush *presets* offer a variety of brush "tips" for creating painterly or special effects. Figure B.5 shows a section of the Options bar, the current presets displayed as *Stroke Thumbnails*, and the menu of other libraries available.

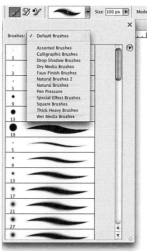

Figure B.5
I won't even mention the control settings under More Options.

Those Stroke Thumbnail samples go from thin to thick and back to thin again. Very natural and convincing. You can only do that with a pressure-sensitive tablet and stylus. Figure B.6 shows my cartoony sketch of a chirping birdie done with a Wacom tablet, and the same sketch attempted with a mouse. Many other tools respond to pressure, so are more manageable with a pressure pen: Eraser, Dodge, Burn, Blur, Clone Stamp, and more. I rest my case.

Figure B.6
Why draw with a bar of soap or a hockey puck?

Gradient Fills

Filling a selection with a gradient requires a click and a drag. The result depends on some choices you make beforehand, and on the length and direction of your drag. There are color presets, the most useful being *Foreground to Background* and *Foreground to Transparent*. Of the five styles available, I tend to use Linear, Radial, and

Reflected. Once again, as with layers and brushes, the usual list of blending modes is available. I'll apply a few gradient fills to the winter forest in Figure B.7.

Figure B.7
Over the river and through the woods to Grandmother's house we go.
(Photo courtesy of Nesa Levy.)

The left section of Figure B.8 has a Foreground to Background linear gradient with purple as foreground color and orange for the background color. I chose Color mode at **100%**, thus changing colors but not affecting the tonal range. I clicked at the top of the image and dragged vertically all the way to the bottom, so the transition of colors occurs about midway.

Figure B.8
Grandmother, what colorful trees you have! What's in this lemonade?

The middle sample has a radial gradient using the Red to Green preset in Difference mode at **100%**. I clicked in the center of the selection and dragged to a corner.

On the right you see the subtle effect of the Foreground to Transparent preset, with purple as the foreground color. Using Color mode at **50%** opacity and the Linear style, I dragged from top to bottom, so the gradient would fade away completely about halfway down.

Clone Stamp

This tool enables you to paint parts of images over other parts. The most practical use is for repair and retouching. Figure B.9 has good ol' Mona before and after I got rid of that ugly green streak above her head. I clicked on a "clean" area of sky nearby with my Option/Alt key down. Then I painted right over the green streak in Normal mode at **100%**.

Figure B.9
Okay, I'm in the public domain, but gimme a break already!

You can use the Clone Stamp for fun as well as profit. Look again at Figure B.9 to find a bit of mischief I made with Aligned turned off. I Option/Alt-clicked on the mouth, then painted one stroke over each eye. If Aligned had been enabled, the second stroke would have come from another part of her face.

Toning Tools

Dodge, *Burn*, and *Sponge* share a space on the Tools palette. Dodge is used to lighten pixels and Burn darkens them. Both give you a choice of range on the Options bar: Shadows, Midtones, or Highlights. Sponge has two modes: *Desaturate* reduces the richness of color, and I'm sure you can guess what *Saturate* does. Look how easy it is to put bags under the lovely eye of the woman in Figure B.10, using these toning tools.

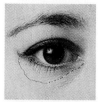

Figure B.10
Getting old in a hurry.
(Photo courtesy of RubberBall.)

I made an irregular selection under the eye with the Lasso tool, to provide a lower edge for the effect. One or two low-opacity strokes with the Burn tool along the edge of the selection created a shadow. A stroke with the Dodge tool just above it added the highlight. Feeling lucky, I repeated the process to make another bag, for matched luggage. The results show the shadows are too saturated, so Sponge came to the rescue, in Desaturate mode.

Text and Effects

The Type tool, partnered with one or more Styles and Effects, is useful for creating an unlimited array of special looks for letterforms. There's a library of Text Effects in the Effects category. A few of those are shown in Figure B.11.

Figure B.11
These work only on a text layer.

I get a kick out of making type look like its name. Figure B.12 has the word "sand" set in a font called "sand" filled with the color of sand. But that wasn't enough. I applied Filter, Noise, Add Noise to get the texture of sand as well.

Figure B.12   **Life's a beach.**

The Fajita font is available from AGFA Monotype. It comes in two flavors, Mild and Picante. Figure B.13 shows the word "hot" in black with no effects. To the right of that is the same text with the *Wow Neon Yellow On* layer style applied. Figure B.14 can help you navigate to the Wow Neon group of Layer Styles in the palette bin.

Figure B.15
Stage directions, perhaps?

Figure B.13   **Some like it hot.**

Figure B.14
Like, WOW!

"Flag Waving" is set in a font called Impact. Tight *leading* (line spacing) works well here. The Wave style warp settings are shown in Figure B.16. Yes, you can have different colors, even different typefaces, on one text layer. Just highlight the letters you want to change by dragging the Type tool over them. Don't use too many different fonts in one text block to avoid a "ransom note" look.

I applied Wow-Chrome Dark from the Wow Chrome set of Layer Styles to the third copy of "hot." I added the word "metal" on the same text layer, so the layer style was applied to the new text automatically.

Figure B.15 has examples of some Warp Text effects. The Squeeze style can also create a stretch effect by using a negative Bend amount. Both words are set in Gadget. "Louder" is set in Palatino and given a Fisheye warp style with Bend set at **–30%** and Horizontal Distortion at **+50%**.

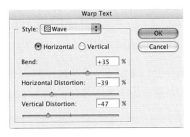

Figure B.16   **That's a warp!**

Differences Between Photoshop Elements and Photoshop CS

The two programs are very similar. Most of the differences are due to Elements being targeted to the consumer market, while CS is designed for graphics professionals. For example, in addition to the traditional image adjustments Elements has several automatic image correction commands in an *Enhance* menu. CS users have to correct images "the hard way." Elements does not have CMYK mode, which is necessary only when preparing images for commercial printing, so that's no biggie for most of us. Elements also lacks *channels* and *paths*. If you've managed to have a normal life without these advanced features so far, chances are you'll continue to do so.

Type tool features are nearly the same in both applications. Only CS offers *kerning* (fine tuning the spaces between letter pairs) and text-on-a-path (since there are no paths in Elements, that's a no-brainer). The *Warp Text* feature, identical in both programs, makes up for the absence of text-on-a–path very nicely. At some point all text has to be converted to pixels, just like any image layer. This command is called *Simplify Layer* in Elements, but CS uses the more technical term, *Rasterize*.

Having always used the full version prior to writing this book, there are just a few things I wished for. The absence of *layer masks* is noticeable. Layer masks allow you to paint areas of a layer in or out of visibility. This is a very powerful feature for controlling how layers interact. We get them for adjustment layers, but not for image layers.

There's no *History Brush* available for Elements. This would allow you to paint back to an earlier stage of an image. As a workaround, which I recommended in a few of the projects, I use a layer that is a copy of the image, leaving the original untouched as the background. That way, I can simply erase where I want the original back again. This difference no doubt accounts for the *Art History Brush*, which shares a space with the *History Brush* on the tools palette, being called (more accurately, I think) the *Impressionist Brush* in Elements.

I also prefer the much greater control over *layer styles* available with CS. There are many more settings for each effect, and you can easily combine layer styles and toggle them on or off in the Layers palette, individually or together.

Finally, only Elements has the *Cookie Cutter tool*! I probably could've done a whole chapter with that little cutie. Maybe I will in the next edition.

Index

J-K

L

These Que and Sams books will help you build your technical skills and enhance the quality of the projects you can create. You'll learn more about Photoshop Elements, digital cameras, and digital photography techniques. When you combine all of your skills, you'll have even more fun with Photoshop Elements 3!

Other Books of Interest

Bad Pics Fixed Quick: How to Fix Lousy Digital Pictures

Michael Miller
ISBN: 0-7897-3209-2 • $24.99 USA

Sams Teach Yourself Adobe Photoshop Elements 3 in a Snap

Jennifer Fulton and Scott M. Fulton
ISBN: 0-672-32668-X • $29.99 USA

Absolute Beginner's Guide to Digital Photography

Joseph Ciaglia, Barbara London, John Upton, and Peter Kuhns
ISBN: 0-7897-3120-7 • $18.99 USA

Sams Teach Yourself Digital Photography and Photoshop Elements 3 All in One

Carla Rose
ISBN: 0-672-32688-4 • $34.99 USA

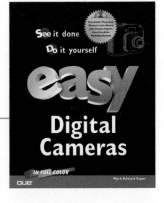

Easy Digital Cameras

Mark Soper
ISBN: 0-7897-3077-4 • $19.99 USA